Acts of the Council of Trent with the Antidote

John Calvin

Monergism Books

CONTENTS

JOHN CALVIN TO THE PIOUS READER.   V

ADMONITION AND EXHORTATION OF THE   VII
LEGATES OF THE APOSTOLIC SEE TO THE FA-
THERS IN THE COUNCIL OF TRENT.

CALVIN'S PREFACE TO THE ANTIDOTE.   XX

ON THE PREFACTORY DISCOURSE BY THE   XXX
LEGATES IN THE FIRST SESSION AND OTHER
PRELIMINARY MATTERS OF THE COUNCIL.

1. DECREE PUBLISHED IN THE SECOND SESSION   1
   OF THE HOLY COUNCIL OF TRENT.

2. ON THE DECREE OF THE SECOND SESSION.   4

3. FIRST DECREE PUBLISHED IN THE THIRD SES-   9
   SION OF THE COUNCIL OF TRENT.

4. ON THE DECREE OF THE THIRD SESSION.   12

5. FIRST DECREE OF THE FOURTH SESSION OF   14
   THE COUNCIL OF TRENT.

6. SECOND DECREE OF THE FOURTH SESSION.   17

7. ON THE FOURTH SESSION   20

8. FIRST DECREE OF THE FIFTH SESSION OF THE   32
    COUNCIL OF TRENT,

9. SECOND DECREE OF THE FIFTH SESSION.   36

10. ON THE FIRST DECREE OF THE FIFTH SESSION.   42

11. ON THE SECOND DECREE OF THE FIFTH SES-   47
    SION.

12. SIXTH SESSION OF THE COUNCIL OF TRENT.   51

13. ON THE SIXTH SESSION OF THE COUNCIL OF   69
    TRENT.

14. SEVENTH SESSION OF THE COUNCIL OF   131
    TRENT.

JOHN CALVIN TO THE PIOUS READER.

I t is said that Cato, when about to address the Roman People for the purpose of urging them to correct their extravagant expenditure, began by premising that he should have a difficult task to perform, as the belly had no ears. My task, were I to exhort the Romanists of the present day to restore the doctrine of godliness, and cleanse the Church of corruption, would be much more difficult: for I should have to contend not only with a deaf belly, but with blind ambition. We seer that however they may be vanquished in argument, they nevertheless continue obstinate because they think they have to fight for honor and life. I will not, therefore, be so foolish as to attempt in vain to recall them to a sound mind; those of them, I mean, whose contumacy is seen to be altogether desperate. I will rather turn in a different direction, and let all the godly see how abominable the impiety of those men is. Of this I here exhibit no obscure specimen in The Acts of the Council of Trent, in which they have so explained all their inward feelings, as to leave, nobody in doubt what the state of the Church would be if it depended on their decision.

But that this may the better appears I beg and exhort my readers first to peruse my treatise on the Necessity of Reforming the Church; and thereafter, on comparing, decide to which party they ought to incline.

GENEVA, 21st November 1547.

ADMONITION AND EXHORTATION OF THE LEGATES OF THE APOSTOLIC SEE TO THE FATHERS IN THE COUNCIL OF TRENT.

R EAD IN THE FIRST SESSION.

Reverend Fathers, etc. — Seeing that the very nature of the office assigned to us, who in this Holy Council perform the part of Presidents and Legates of the Apostolic See, seems to demand that, amid the multiplicity of business to be dispatched in this sacred assembly to the glory of God and the good of the Church, we should repeatedly address you by way of exhortation and admonition; more especially have we thought it right not to omit so to do in this first Session, which will, we hope, give a happy commencement to the whole Council. And we perform this duty the more willingly, because, while we either exhort you to act worthily of this great assembly, or dissuade you from the contrary, we also exhort and dissuade ourselves, who are as it were in the same vessel with you, exposed to the same perils and the same storms; we say, we excite ourselves to watch, that we may neither fall among rocks, numbers of which will doubtless appear during this voyage, nor by our negligence allow the magnitude of the business to overwhelm us like waves of the sea; but, sustained by faith and hope, may guide the vessel in that special direction where a haven of safety shall appear to the glory of God in Jesus Christ.

Therefore, to begin with that of which, particularly at the outset, we ought also to be reminded, each one of us ought to place in his view, first of all, what the things are which are expected from this sacred Council. Thereby each will easily understand how great a burden lies upon him. Now, the things expected (to embrace them all summarily) are those contained in the Bull calling the Council, namely, The Extirpation of Heresies, The Restoration of Ecclesiastical Discipline and Reformation of Manners, and, finally, The External Peace of the whole Church. These, therefore, are the things for which it behooves us to care, or which we ought constantly to pray that God would of his goodness grant.

And there is one thing of which, above all, at the very outset of the Council, we have thought that all, collectively and individually, who have here assembled, and especially we ourselves who preside in this sacred function, ought to be admonished — never to imagine that, either by the individuals here present: or by the whole Council, were all the Pastors throughout the world here met, could a cure be provided for the great evils by which the flock of Christ is now oppressed. If we think that this can be accomplished by us, or by any other than Christ himself, whom God the Father hath given to be our only Savior and Pastor, to whom also he hath given all power, we certainly err at the very foundation in all our doings, and shall still further provoke the Divine anger. For to the former evils which have befallen us, because we have forsaken the very fountain of living water, we add the other very grievous sin of wishing to cure those evils by our own power or skill, so that what the Prophet says in the name of God, accusing his ancient people, might justly be said of us — This people hath committed two evils; they have forsaken me, the fountain of living water, and hewn out to themselves cisterns not fit to contain water. Such cisterns are all the counsels which proceed from our own wisdom, uninspired by the Divine Spirit. Such counsels not only are not able to keep the people in piety and obedience, like water in cisterns; but the more we labor to confirm them by these devices, the more violently do they, like torrents, flow from us, and go away, as the experience of former years, in many places, may sufficiently teach; while it now reminds us that only one method of curing these evils remains — if, acknowledging that all our remedies are useless, and are fitter to increase evils than to take them away, we, who hold the place of Fathers, do in all things flee in faith and hope to the power of Christ, whom God the Father calls his right hand, and to the wisdom of Christ, which is the wisdom of the Father, acknowledging ourselves to be in all things his servants. Moreover, (says the Apostle,) it is required of stewards that a man be found faithful. (1 Corinthians 4:2.) What must now be done, is in all things to show ourselves fit servants. And we shall be fit, if we judge that of ourselves we are by no means fit. For who, says the same Apostle, is sufficient for these things? And therefore we are not to think anything of ourselves, as if of ourselves we were sufficient.

But it is not enough for us thus to confess. The Apostle could say, that by this gate he entered in to fulfill his office, and that he therein showed himself a fit and faithful minister; for he could at the same time say, I am conscious to myself of nothing. But we, if we will confess the truth, cannot but say that, in administering the office assigned us, we are conscious of having failed in very many things, and have in no small degree been the cause of those evils which we are met to correct. For as it is not enough to confess that we are unequal to so great an office, what more must we do in order to be at this time the fit ministers of Christ in renewing the Church? The same thing undoubtedly which Christ himself, the Bishop of our souls, did when he came to found and form his Church. The same thing assuredly, Fathers, must we do which the very Wisdom of the Father did, when he came to lead many sons unto glory. This is the thing at which we ought now to aim. For he, seeing all men overwhelmed in sin, took the sins of all upon himself, and made himself alone guilty and condemned before God for all, and bore the penalty due by us, as if he had himself committed all the iniquities and crimes of which we had been guilty; whereas he was perfectly free from all taint of sin, inasmuch as he did no sin, neither was guile found in his mouth. What Christ thus did, out of boundless love, towards God the Father, and pity towards our race, justice itself now demands that we shall do, in order that we pastors may not stand guilty before the tribunal of the divine mercy of all those evils by which the flock of Christ is oppressed, and, transferring the sins of all to ourselves, not so much from pity as justice, because in truth we are in a great measure the cause of these evils, implore the divine mercy through Jesus Christ. When we said that we pastors have given occasion to the evils by which the Church is oppressed, should any one think the language exaggerated, and more strongly than truly expressed, experience, which cannot lie, will prove its truth.

Let us look then for a little to the evils by which the Church is oppressed, and at the same time to our sins. But these who can number? Along with other evils, they are more than the sand of the sea, and cry aloud to heaven. Let us therefore circumscribe the multitude of our sins within those limits within which this Council summoned to cure the worst of evils has circumscribed them. These, as we have mentioned above, are three, viz., heresies, decay of discipline, intestine and external war. Here, then, let us see and consider, since the Church has been now for many years vexed with these calamities, in what sources they had their origin — whether we did not in some measure begin — whether we have not fomented them.

First, let us examine the beginning of the Heresies which have everywhere sprung up in this our day. Should we deny that we gave a beginning to them because we ourselves have not been the authors of any heresy, still, inasmuch as perverse opinions concerning faith are a kind of brambles and thorns which have sprung up in the field of the Lord, given to us to cultivate, although these have risen of their own accord, as weeds are sometimes wont to do, yet he who has not cultivated the field as he ought — who has not sown it — who, as the weeds sprung up spontaneously, has not been careful to extirpate them, may be said to have given them a beginning, just as if he had sown them, especially considering that they all derive their origin and increase from the carelessness of the husbandman. Here, then, let those who are husbandmen in the Lord's field examine themselves, let them ask their conscience how they have acted in cultivating and in sowing. Those who have done so, especially in these times in which very few labor in cultivating the field of the Lord, have, we presume, little doubt that to themselves belongs the blame of the heresies which have grown rank in every part of the Church. But enough has been said by way of admonition concerning the evils which belong to the first head.

Let us come to the second, which relates to The Decay of Discipline, and what are called Abuses. Here it is of no use to spend time in inquiring who were the authors of those great evils, since beside ourselves no others can be named.

Let us therefore proceed to the third head, which relates to The Obstacles to the Peace of the Church, such as wars, domestic or foreign. For these long ago disturbed the peace of the Church, and disturb it still. Here we only say, that if war be (as God has shown by infallible signs) the scourge by which he chastises us, then as we are guilty under the two former heads, in regard to which we cannot excuse ourselves, so we cannot deny that we are the principal cause of those wars. Such scourges, we presume, God sends in order to chastise us as sinners, and set before our eyes the very sins by which we have most grievously offended his majesty. Here let every one who has observed in what way the Church has been vexed by warlike violence, consider with himself what those things are in which the Church thereby suffers loss. Nor does it matter here of what kind of warfare we speak — whether of the intestine wars of our own princes, or the foreign wars of Turks, which of late years have brought great calamities upon us, or of the wars of those who have thrown off obedience to their pastors, and driven them from their sees. What we say applies in general to all kinds of warfare, including that of those who have wielded weapons against us — have banished pastors from their churches — confounded orders — substituted laymen in the room of bishops — plundered the property of the Church, and obstructed the course of the Word of God. Here we say, that if those who claim the name of pastors will but read what is contained in the book on the abuses of pastors, the greater part of them will find it stated, in express terms, that they have themselves committed them. For they will find that our ambition, our avarice, our passions first brought those evils on the people of God. Owing to them pastors were driven from their churches, and churches deprived of the nurture of the Word; the property of churches, which is the property of the poor, was taken from them; the priests office was conferred on unworthy persons, and given to those differing in no respect from laity except in dress, and not even in this. Which of these things can we deny that we have done in recent years? Wherefore if the Turk, if heretics do the very same against us, what else do we behold than our own flagrant misdeeds, and at the same time see the just judgment of God — a judgment, however, fraught with mercy? For had he chastised us according to our deservings, we should long ago have been as Sodom and as Gomorrah.

But why do we now bring these things to mind? Is it for your confusion? Far from it. It is rather to admonish you as dear fathers and brethren, and first of all admonish ourselves how we may be able to avoid the scourges which now chastise us, and the severer scourges impending, unless we repent, that we may escape the dreadful judgment of God — dreadful indeed to all the impenitent, but especially to those who rule. Those who rule, says Scripture, will be severely judged. We see that judgment now begins at the house of God. While priests are cast out and trampled under feet of men, what else is indicated but the Divine judgment upon us, which our Savior foretold when he said that his priests are the salt of the earth, but if the salt hath lost its savor, it is good for nothing but to be cast out and trodden under feet of men? All these things we now suffer. If it were for righteousness' sake, like our forefathers, happy were we; but now it is justly, because the salt has lost its savor. We do not at all suffer for righteousness' sake; for in all our afflictions we see the just judgment of God. Would, indeed, that we did see it; for this were the first step of escape from all the judgments and chastisements of God, and of entrance into favor and true glory.

It is this that has made us longer and stricter in calling these things to mind. For unless these things be known, and thoroughly understood, in vain do we enter the Council, in vain do we invoke the Holy Spirit, who always makes His first entrance into the soul of man by condemning the man himself, that He may convict the world of sin. Wherefore, unless that Spirit have first condemned us to ourselves, we may be assured that he has not entered into us, and will not even enter if we refuse to listen to our sins. For the same thing will be said to us which was said to the ancient people by the Prophet Ezekiel, when without acknowledging their sins, they wished to inquire at God through the Prophet. The Prophet speaks thus, — "The children of Israel came to me to inquire at the Lord, and sat before me. But thus saith the Lord, Have you come to inquire at me? As I live, saith the Lord, I will not answer you. And he adds, "If you judge them, show them the abominations of their fathers." In these words God shows why he refused to answer them, viz., because they had not yet listened to their own abominations and those of their fathers. Wherefore, seeing the Divine Spirit who then gave responses is the same whom we now invoke, while sitting before the Lord, you see what we have to do to procure a proper answer, and at the same time how necessary it was for us who preside in this sacred assembly to employ our first address in laying open our sins.

But as we now see some grievously lamenting, first their own sins and those of our order, and with earnest prayer imploring the Divine mercy, we have the strongest hopes that the Spirit of God, whom we invoke, has come to us. For we regard as the grand pledge of the Divine mercy, this very commencement of the Council in which we are now convened to raise up and renovate the almost fallen Church, as the ancient people, after their long captivity among foreign princes, returned to Jerusalem to rebuild the Temple. In the state of that people, in their joyful departure for their native land, and the rebuilding of the Temple, we may behold an image of our own time and state, especially in this Council, and in the example of the leaders of that people, You who are leaders of the people of God on their way to the heavenly country, see your duty. Wherefore, we strongly exhort all of you often to call to mind what is written in the Books of Ezra, and Nehemiah, and Daniel, in which the counsels of all the leaders of the people are unfolded, as having always had this one end in view, viz., by confessing their own sins and those of the people, to stir up all to repentance and supplication for the Divine mercy. When the people did so, everything went well with them. If we would expect success, and a happy issue in rebuilding the Church, for which cause we have here gladly assembled, we must follow the same counsels, and this the more, because greater contests await us in rebuilding the Church than they had in rebuilding the Temple. For if many opposed them to prevent the accomplishment of the work, and many, too, when they could not prevent it, derided, rest assured that we too shall not be without mockers, and others who will do their utmost to call us off, and deter us from our undertaking. We shall have to wrestle not only with flesh and blood, but with spiritual wickednesses in high places. But He in whose name we have engaged in the work is more powerful than they. "Wherefore, let us trust in him, let us call upon him in prayer, and he will bring all things to pass.

But as this Council is intended both for deliberation and judgment, as we are both to deliberate concerning the things which pertain to the good of the whole Church, and judge as well of things as of persons, (for we sit as it were judging the twelve tribes of Israel, in which is comprehended the whole people of God,) this seems the most proper place for admonishing ourselves, to beware of those things which usually impair the faculties both of deliberation and judgment. These are the passions of the mind, and are also termed perturbations, because they disturb the judgment and feelings, and pervert them from what is right and true. Among these things we must specially guard against those which a heathen historian rightly discards from counsel when he says, "All men consulting on dubious matters should be free from anger, hatred, and friendship." To such passions all mankind are prone, but those are particularly so who are in the service of princes; for they are under stronger affections, and most readily speak from favor or hatred, no doubt, as they think the princes themselves affected, to whom they look for reward. When we speak of princes we mean as well those called ecclesiastical as those who are secular; and though we acknowledge and are glad that we have Christian princes, a privilege which in ancient times, when the Church was newly founded, our fathers had not, still it must before all things be observed by us in this Council, that this is not the place for praising any one but God alone, in Jesus Christ, justifying him only, and condemning every class of men, and first of all ourselves who thus speak, so that we should say with Daniel,

"To us belongs confusion of face; to our kings, our princes, and our fathers, who have sinned; but to thee our Lord God, mercy and forgiveness; for we have forsaken thee, and not listened to the voice of the Lord our God, to walk in the law which he hath given us by his servants the Prophets. And all Israel have broken thy law, and turned aside from hearkening to thy voice, and curse and detestation have descended upon us." (Daniel 9:8-11.)

This is perhaps the place where, after the example of the same Prophet whose words we have just quoted, we who are priests should not only confess our own sins, but those of the people and the princes, before God and his Church, and implore pardon for all. For Daniel speaks thus, — "When I was yet speaking and praying, and confessing my own sins and the sins of my people" — under the name of people in this place comprehending people of all ranks, as his confession just quoted declares. In this matter he seems plainly to intimate what we who have come hither for the safety of the whole Church, now suffering from so many evils, have to do, namely, with tears to confess our own sins, and also those of the princes and people, as we now do abundantly in the spirit of sorrow, but would do more exuberantly in words, were the princes themselves present to join us with their confession and their tears. But in such matters the sins of the priests, and princes, and people also, are bound together, as the Prophets express it, as with a rope of sins, so that it is difficult to inquire into the sins of one class, without at the same time making manifest the sins of other classes. Hence Ezekiel, accusing all classes in one continued discourse, thus speaks in the name of God among his ancient people. "Their priests have despised my law, and polluted my sanctuary. Their princes in the midst of them, like ravening wolves, in shedding blood, destroying souls, and greedily following after lucre, have made no distinction between sacred and profane. The nations of the earth uttered calumny." Would that these words were applicable to those times only, and did not exhibit an image of our own! Would that when we speak of the corruption of priests, we were able to affirm that princes and people have not given the greatest occasion, the largest materials and sanction to it! But let us now reserve our words for a more reasonable time, and open fountains of common tears.

We now return to those whom we have taken it upon us to admonish, especially the Bishops who have come hither with mandates from princes. Our advice to them is to serve their princes with all fidelity and diligence, but, as becomes bishops, to serve as the servants of God and not as the servants of men. Be unwilling, says the Apostle, to be the servants of men. First, let them serve the one King Christ, to whom God the Father hath given all power; next, for his sake let them serve all, and especially their princes, giving honor to whom honor is due, tribute to whom tribute. And we exhort them to serve their princes in regard to honor, as they bear their commands in words in which nothing almost is proposed but what is honorable and aims at the public good. In one word, let them so serve as aiming especially at the honor of God and the utility of this Council, which has been convened for the public good. Wherefore as we most earnestly exhort all who are to give their opinions here before God and his angels and the whole Church, not to speak for the favor of any man, so much more do we exhort them not to utter a sentence from hatred of any man, though he bear the character of an opponent, or hater, or an open foe.

In fine, it is our earnest wish and exhortation in the Lord, that we abstain from all strife among ourselves. For these are the things which grieve and repel the Holy Spirit whom we have invoked, and without whom we shall not be able to do anything at all for the good and peace of the Church. For, says the Apostle, seeing there are contentions among you, are you not men and do you not walk after man? In calling them men, he means that they are devoid of the Spirit of God.

But in all things which pertain to The Reformation of the Church, (the object for which we have met,) it behooves us to imitate him who formed it at first, of whom, when entering upon his work, the prophet in the name of God thus speaks: "Behold my servant whom I have chosen, my beloved in whom my soul is well pleased; I have sent my Spirit upon him, he will announce judgment to the Gentiles: he will not contend, nor cry. The bruised reed he will not break, the smoking flax he will not quench." This Spirit of peace, charity, and meekness, as we ought always to show before all and with all, so more especially in this sacred assembly in which we have met, that by the grace of the Spirit himself an end may be put to the contentions which have too long vexed the Church. Wherefore we who bear the office of peacemakers must be particularly careful not to give any one any handle for contention. This and all other inconveniences and hinderances shall we avoid by the only means of peace, and we shall arrive at the wished for haven of peace, if with prayers sent from humble and contrite hearts we beseech the Spirit of Christ, who is our peace, to preside in this Council, to pour light into our hearts, and overrule and direct us in all things to his own honor and the real good of the Church. For to such he himself says: "While you yet speak, lo! I am present." Wherefore, we entreat you in the Lord to be constant in such prayers with all possible charity, that with one mouth and one spirit we may glorify God the Father in Jesus Christ, who is God blessed for ever. AMEN.

CALVIN'S PREFACE TO THE ANTIDOTE.

T he name of Sacred Council is held in such reverence in the Christian Church, that the very mention of it produces an immediate effect not only on the ignorant but on men of gravity and sound judgment. And doubtless, as the usual remedy which God employed from the beginning in curing the diseases of his Church was for pious and holy pastors to meet, and, after invoking his aid, to determine what the Holy Spirit dictated, Councils are deservedly honored by all the godly. There is this difference, however, — the vulgar, stupified with excessive admiration, do not afterwards make any use of their judgment, whereas those of sounder sense allow themselves, step by step, and modestly, indeed, but still allow themselves to inquire before they absolutely assent. And so it ought to be, in order that our faith, instead of rashly subscribing to the naked decisions of men, may submit to God only.

This is objected to by those who are persuaded, or at least would persuade others:, that no Council whatever, provided it have been duly called, can err — inasmuch as it is guided by the Holy Spirit. Accordingly they insist that everything proceeding from it shall be received, like an oracle, without controversy. How much wiser is Augustine who, from his singular modesty, indeed bestows no small honor upon Councils, and yet ceases not to observe the moderation which I have described. Writing against the Arian, Maximinus, he says: "I ought neither to adduce the Council of Nice, nor you that of Ariminum, as if to prejudge the question. I am not determined by the authority of the latter, nor you by that of the former. Founding on the authority of Scripture not peculiar to either, but the common witness of both, fact contends with fact, plea with plea, reason with reason." So much liberty does this holy man concede to himself and others, that he will not allow the Council of Nice to operate as a previous judgment, unless the truth of the case be plainly established from Scripture.

But there is no occasion at present to dwell longer on these Ancient Councils. I have to treat of The Council of Trent, which was of a very different description. When many corruptions were seen in the Church, when grave disputes on doctrine had arisen, a Council was long and ardently desired by many who hoped that by this means all evils would be ended. In this, indeed, they erred. For as matters are at present constituted, those possessed of any discernment easily perceive that no alleviation of evils is to be hoped from those who have the power of calling and holding a Council. Still as no better method appeared, very many persons not ill-disposed, who wished well to the Church, anticipated some good from a Council. Accordingly, being desired by many, it was at length demanded, as it were, by the common voice of Christendom.

Of the causes which delayed it for a considerable time, the more discerning are aware. For as to those causes which the Roman Pontiff alleges in his Bull, whosoever does not see them to be impudent fictions is more than blind. The causes which induced him to weave all possible delays, he himself best knows; and yet we can in some measure conjecture. Some think he was afraid lest the Council might as a kind of vulgar thing be held cheap, both by princes and people, if it were at once so easily obtained. For long expectation, provided it does not tire out men's patience, usually adds a new value to things. I think, however, that there was a different reason. Although he knew that the Council which he would give would be nothing else than a hired crew of his own followers, among whom he himself alone would be eminent; still, such is the power of an evil conscience, that he trembled at the very mention of a Council. For with such dissolute and unbridled license is the Papal tyranny exercised, that those who are most desirous to preserve it in being, have no doubt as to the necessity of curbing it. Hence, not without cause, he endeavored by spinning out the time to escape from any diminution of his power. This afterwards appeared still more clearly; for all the steps which he took in ordering his Council, contrary to the received custom, are so many proofs of the distrust which I have mentioned. To omit an infinite number of other things, why were three legates sent but just that they might operate as mutual checks, and each prevent the other from attempting anything? In his own band, though they are all his sworn serfs, he found none whom he could trust.

Such were the private views of the Pope. A different view was taken by those who are unwilling that the present state of the Church, be it what it may, should be disturbed. They held that anything was better than to enter on a regular discussion of the subjects debated in the present day. Why so? Partly because it seems to them unbecoming to raise discussion, in any form, as to human decrees which have once been received; partly because violent possession delights them more than free government in any shape. For how few are those who now defend the

Papacy under the pretext of zeal for the Church, who do not desire the liberty of the Christian people to be so crushed, that no one may dare a whisper about correcting the vices of the Church, or who do not clamor that a Council is needless, and that atrocious injustice is done to prior decisions, if they are not adhered to without any mention of a Council. What else is this, they ask, but to do what has been already done? And what license will be given in future to innovation and disturbance, if we do not acquiesce in things once decided? If the decisions already given are oracles of the Holy Spirit, what can be gained by new discussion? All this is easily refuted. Questions are agitated in the present day which were never before duly discussed; and it is plain that both the doctrine and the whole administration of the Papacy are so much at variance with the majority of ancient Councils, that nothing more opposite can be imagined. Moreover, the diseases under which the Church labors are so various and deadly, that at no period was it ever more necessary to hold a Council, if indeed there were any hope that a lawful Council could be obtained. It is apparent, therefore, that those who thus speak have not the least sense of true piety, but at ease, and almost with joy, contemplate the miserable distraction of the Church. Their assertion, that matters which have once been decided cannot again be lawfully agitated, is too absurd. For in this view, wherein does the Holy Word of God differ from the decrees of man? If they would go back for their authorities to those purer ages which were distinguished for learning and piety, they might perhaps be listened to; but the Councils by whose decisions they wish to fetter us are those in which nothing but the grossest ignorance appears, united to barbarian ferocity. That this is strictly true will be made plain in its proper place. It furnishes the true reason for their talking so loudly of final judgments already pronounced.

Moreover, if hithero there was any doubt how great the difference is between a Council and the tribunal of the Holy Spirit, from which there is no appeal, a striking illustration has been given us in The Council of Trent. They contend that a Council cannot err, because it represents the Church. What if the latter position be denied to be true? But in order to determine the point we must, I presume, see who the men are that compose it. Perhaps forty Bishops or so are present. I do not keep to a number, nor much care about it, as it is of little consequence. Let the advocates of Councils answer me in good faith. Were any one to review them all in order, how many of them would he not contemn? Nay, when the venerable Fathers look in each other's faces, it must be impossible for them not to feel ashamed; for they know themselves, and are not ignorant of the opinion which they have of each other. Hence, if you take away the name of Council, the whole Papacy will confess that all the bishops who attended were nothing but dregs.

I am willing, however, to let other nations keep their ornaments untouched. I will only ask my French countrymen what price they set on the portion which they contributed? They doubtless hold the kingdom of France to be one of the leading branches of the Church. Why, then, it sent but two bishops, one from Nantes, and another from Clermont, both equally dull and unlearned. The latter was not long ago deemed as ridiculous as a buffoon, and so libidinous, that he was wont to track out dens of infamy with the scent of a pointer, till he placed himself under the discipline of a notorious Parisian, Sosia. After this he became suddenly wise, if men can so easily be, made wise by a lady of the school of Francis Picart. It is clear that the master is completely devoid of brains, belongs to the class of fanatics, and is little better than a madman. The Archbishop of Aix I scarcely count a Frenchman. He of Asti, however, as is usual with curious men, was present as an idle spectator. I ask you, my countrymen, who among you can persuade himself that anything which even a countless multitude of such men could have vented proceeded from the Holy Spirit? The two of whom I speak never had a taste of even the first rudiments of theology. How miserable, then, will the condition of the Christian Church be, if everything which pleased them, and a few no better than they, is to be held oracular! And yet very many are so thoughtless, that when they hear of the publication of the Decrees of the Holy Council, they reflect not that the authors of them are persons to whom they would not give the least credit in the paltriest question. Did this occur to them they would instantly reject with indignation and trample under foot what they now inconsiderately kiss. Why? Is there anything which their judgment approves? Not at all. But reverence for the Council blinds them. What folly, when you knew the ass to tremble at his lion's skin!

But here it may be objected by the opposite party, that the decision did not rest with the bishops alone. I am aware. And this I particularly wished to observe. For there are certain garrulous and audacious monks, some of whom hunt after mitres, and others after cardinals' hats, while all of them sell their prattle to the Roman Pontiff. Let us assume, however, that they are excellent persons, and theologians of no common erudition. This, however, I know, that the venerable Fathers, on whose nod all religion depends, are preceded verbally by a set of sophists whose *dicta* they afterwards chant. What end then does it serve for them to mount a lofty seat, and then like demigods give out what a lower bench has dictated? Where is that representation of the Church to which they bind the Holy Spirit, if they are compelled precariously to borrow elsewhere what they need — if they would not be silent or speak in error? Your axiom is, that whatever be the meeting to which you give the name of Universal Council, there the Holy Spirit presides, and nothing can proceed from it that is not heavenly and divine. Meanwhile, you appoint hungry, venal-tongued monks, to whom this fancied spirit of yours must listen. They, in long and formal discussions, debate whatever is to be defined by the fathers: so I have heard; they keep quarreling and croaking away like the frogs of Aristophanes. At length those famous decrees are concocted and afterwards given out as the responses of the Holy Spirit. And why should I misrepresent in a matter which is perfectly notorious? It is certain that there is no school so obscure as not to look down with contempt on anything coming from the theologians of Trent. What then? Shall we think that the moment they have changed their place, they receive a sudden afflatus., as if, like the priestesses of Apollo, they had entered the Delphian cauldron? Absurd! Were it to be announced today to the Sorbonne at Paris, that the Fathers of Trent differed in one iota from their decisions, the brains of its doctors would instantly warm, and they would rush forth to the combat. Not only would they set the authority of the Council at nought, but assail every man of them by name with the fiercest invectives. But here, if they give a white ball in support of their absurdest dreams, all the schools of France, Spain, Germany, and Italy will vie in applause. How dishonest then to obtrude and call upon the Christian world to worship that which they in their hearts utterly disregard!

But suppose we assume that those disputants who sweat in forging decrees are not only wondrously acute and learned, but are angels just come down from heaven; and suppose we also pardon our opponents the great absurdity of holding that a Council, which they proudly affirm to be guided by the immediate inspiration of the Spirit, goes a begging to a few individuals for that which it sends over the whole world as of divine origin — not even thus will the Council of Trent obtain a particle of credit. For nothing is determined there save at the nod of the Roman

Pontiff. In future, then, let them have done with their bombast, that he who rejects the decrees of the Council fights not with men but with God — that they are nothing but instruments, while he is the President who guides their minds and tongues by his Spirit. Were it so, I hold that they themselves insult the Holy Spirit by reprimanding him through their Pope, to whose decision and censure everything is subjected. I speak of what is perfectly notorious. As soon as any decree is framed, couriers flee off to Rome, and beg pardon and peace at the feet of their idol. The holy father hands over what the couriers have brought to his private advisers for examination. They curtail, add, and change as they please. The couriers return, and a sederunt is appointed. The notary reads over what no one dares to disapprove, and the asses shake their ears in assent. Behold the oracle which imposes religious obligations on the whole world! Why do they not openly confess the thing as it is — that ten or twenty monks, whose labors they have hired, concoct the decrees — that the Pope puts his censorial pen through whatever does not please him, and approves of the rest — that nothing is left to the Council but the burden of publishing? In ancient times, after the Roman Senate had deliberated, the plebeians examined; but the Pope, by no means contented with examining, arrogates right, moreover, to correct anything that does not please him in the deliberation of the Council. Presumptuously does he so act, if he thinks that the Holy Spirit is presiding there. We, however, I presume, may with impunity despise it, because we are aware of its being composed by such doctors, and corrected by such an Aristarchus. The proclamation of the Council is entitled to no more weight than the cry of an auctioneer.

But not to preface longer, should I, while trusting to the sure testimony of the Word of God, call the decrees of a Council in question, methinks I have proved that there is no reason why sober readers should

charge me with presumption. But now, who that is not more than fatuous can be angry with me, when compelled by the necessity of maintaining the truth, I hesitate not to expose an ape though adorned with purple
and let all see him to be the ape he is? I have already amply shown that
those Neptunian fathers are not so formidable with their Trident as that
one may not boldly flagellate them with the Word of God, nor so sacred
as to make it impious to touch them. But to my view that is not now
the question. The mask which the Roman Pontiff has placed on the eyes
of men is one by which no seeing man can be deceived. When, ten years
ago, a Council was everywhere talked of, and the belief accordingly was,
that the Pope could no longer by equivocation escape from collecting his
flocks in good earnest, and bulls of citation had begun to fly about, I for
my part conjectured that the summonses founded on the bulls would
gradually go off into smoke. For I remembered another bull of Mantua,
under the pontificate of Pius II., which, after much swelling talk, had
instantly vanished. But if a Council were at length to be assembled, I
considered with myself that the Roman Pontiff would use every means
to dazzle the eyes of the simple with no ordinary splendor: and, to confess
the truth, this thought made me exceedingly anxious. As to one thing
there was no doubt, viz., that whoever should be allowed to sit and give
their opinion, all of them, some ensnared by ambition, others blinded
by avarice, others inflamed with rage, would be mortal enemies to sound
doctrine, and being bound together in secret conspiracy to establish the
tyranny of the Pope, would exert themselves to destroy the kingdom
of Christ. There might, perhaps, be a very few unaffected by this cruel
and impious feeling, but still without the manliness to resist it in others.
I therefore immediately concluded, that under such unjust judges, the
truth would be oppressed without being heard. For it was not even to be
hoped that any one pious and right-hearted man would venture, at the

expense of his life, to purchase one hour's audience. Meanwhile many unskillful, though otherwise honest persons would be imposed upon, by the plausible axiom that the decision of the Church must be acquiesced in. Thanks to the Pope for furnishing us with a display which our very children will hold in derision! I ask nothing of my readers, however, but to lay prejudice in favor of either party aside, and come unbiassed to the discussion. This they can only do by withdrawing their eye from persons, and fixing it on the subject.

ON THE PREFACTORY DISCOURSE BY THE LEGATES IN THE FIRST SESSION AND OTHER PRELIMINARY MATTERS OF THE COUNCIL.

I t is well! At length the Romanists confess, that the fearful distraction of the Church at present, which all good men deplore, is in a great measure attributable to themselves. Any one, not very shrewd, on hearing this candid confession, will forthwith conceive good hopes. And the exhortations which follow exhibit no ordinary zeal for the renovation of the Church. Thus, that part in which they declare that none can succor their falling affairs save Christ the only Shepherd, that therefore they must implore and listen to him alone; that all will go prosperously if he guides all their actions and presides, over them; that all other counsels, other arts, are but leaky cisterns which let out water; that the wisdom of man does nought but further provoke the anger of God, and increase evils rather than cure them — of all that part, I say — how strongly it breathes of piety! But it is apparent from the acts which followed, that those were vain words given to the winds. Nay, they do not wait till a judgment is formed from their acts. For in regard to the doctrine of salvation, which they have wholly adulterated by their impious and abominable fictions; in regard to the sacraments which they have utterly vitiated, and which they prostitute to a vile and shameless trafficking, they find nothing in themselves to correct. How little aid, then, do they bring to ruined affairs! And truly we can expect nothing from the Tridentines who serve under Neptune but what is of a watery nature, when the business to be undertaken is the Reformation of the Church. But when persecution is to rage against the innocent, and impious tyranny is to be confirmed by the blood of the godly, they at once blaze into flame. Indeed, something resembling this may be seen within the realm of Neptune, when with roaring noise he lashes the waves into foam. Soon, however, it bursts by its own tumescence, and the uproar immediately subsides. They, in like manner, as soon as the smoke has cleared away from their forehead, show without disguise what the nature of their conduct is to be in regard to the principal head. They are to cling with a death-grasp to all their impieties, while we who desire nothing but the reign of Christ, and maintain the pure doctrine of the Gospel, are to be judged heretics. For thus, before cognisance is taken, they declare all heretical who have dared at this time to move a whit against the received doctrine of the Roman Church. What is this? The whole Christian world was in expectation of a Council in which controverted points might be regularly discussed. These men avow that they sit for no other end than to condemn whatever is not to their mind. Therefore, let no man any longer deceive himself: From their own mouths we hear that this pompous Council is held not for inquiry, but to establish that kind of doctrine, be it what it may, with which monks and sophists have imbued the world; that all rites shall remain by whatever superstition they may have crept in; and all the fetters of conscience be drawn into a tighter knot.

Can any one still be so stupid as to think of seeking any alleviation of our evils from a Council? We complain that the whole doctrine of godliness is adulterated by impious dogmas; that the whole worship of God is vitiated by foul and disgraceful superstitions; that the pure institution of the sacraments has been supplanted by horrible sacrilege; that their use has been converted into a profane trafficking; that poor souls, which ought to have been ruled by the doctrine of Christ, are oppressed by cruel bondage; that nothing is seen in the Christian Church that is not deformed and debased; that the grace of Christ not only lies half-buried, but is partly torn to pieces, partly altogether extinguished. All these complaints, which we have made for many years, and in published books, and which we make in our daily sermons, we are prepared to prove well founded, whenever a freedom of utterance is given. Such is the goodness of our cause, that it does not at all fear the light. And many are the tens of thousands so firmly persuaded of it, that they desired no farther investigation. Still, lest the Christian world might lay aside dissension, and unite in holy concord, a Council is summoned. Ought not its members to have discussed controverted points before they prejudged either themselves or others? They allow nothing of the kind. Nay, should any one have attempted to change one tittle of their customs, they hold him as already condemned.

Behold the specious Reformation, with the promise of which they have hitherto amused the world! The many portentous idolatries by which the Church of God is deformed — the many defilements of superstitions — the many profanations of sacred things — the vast sink of errors must not be touched. There is to be no diminution of the tyrannical yoke of impious laws by which miserable consciences have been ensnared; but all who desire any change are to be judged heretics. Where is that hearing which many were simple enough to promise themselves? If religion had any hold of their minds, nay, if they had any belief of a God, would they so confidently, and, as it were, in jest, skip over matters of so much moment? The glory of God is in question, the everlasting kingdom of Christ, the safety of the whole Church. They are compelled, in compliance so far with the common wishes of the Christian people, to hold a Council. They, however, premise, that they come for the very purpose of cutting off all hope of reform. For these words are the same in effect as if they had plainly and distinctly declared that the future would be no better than the past. And yet in thus acting they exhibit nothing foreign to their character. For in the overthrow of piety and the corruptions of sacred things, which in the present day all good men deplore, there is nothing of which those men who sit as judges do not deserve the blame. Do we wonder, then, if, while they themselves are the accused parties, they proceed forthwith, without touching the cause, to pass sentence in their own favor? It is more than absurd to leave the power of judging to those whose criminality is under discussion. And yet, what do they gain, but just to make all who have eyes aware that they do not in the least repent of their crimes while they pertinaciously defend everything of which we accuse them? They will not succeed, however, in getting a sanction to their impiety, because they are themselves obstinate.

Some one will now ask, What then do they hold forth as the benefits to be derived from a Council? To put an end to wars among Christian princes and give tranquility to the Church. Folly! For who knows not that the Romanists are bellows which fan the flame of warlike commotions wherever their blast is applied? The only thing remaining, therefore, is to restore lapsed discipline, especially in their own clergy. With what faith they have exerted themselves in this direction is apparent from their acts; for they there, as we shall see, open up a way by which everything which has been allowed in time past is to be allowed in future. But to prevent it being thought that after all this costly show nothing has been done, there will, perhaps, be some reformation in caps and shoes, and other parts of dress. While they in this way mock God and men, they are not ashamed to personate the Prophets, as if the three Legates of Antichrist were the three intercessors of whom Ezekiel speaks, who first threw themselves into the breach to appease the anger of God. They make an humble confession of sins — they mention groans and tears, the signs of repentance. I believe the person employed as their reader on this occasion must have found it difficult to keep from laughing.

But while they wish to act as players, one expression escapes from them, which I think should be regarded as a divine prediction; for, like Caiaphas of old, what is to prevent the enemies of Christ from prophesying? They declare that the Holy Spirit is not present with them if they do not accuse themselves; they say that he will not be present so long as they refuse to listen to their sins. I receive the oracle. Afterwards, indeed, to give eclat to their assembly, they falsely state that they see tears. But while the case itself proclaims that they remained obstinate in establishing the kingdom of impiety, we believe, according to their prediction, that nothing governed them less than the Holy Spirit. And who sees not that they were forced, against their inclination, by the secret impulse of God, as if they had been put to the question, to make this confession? They adduce Ezekiel as a witness, who declares that God will not answer the people if they do not first acknowledge their own abominations and those of their fathers. Where, then, is such an acknowledgment on their part? Let them be silent, then, or confess that they send forth the figments of their own brain at random, But if I have not yet convinced all men of this, at least let the reader remember, that when we come to discussion, truth itself must decide whether their decrees proceeded from the inspiration of the Holy Spirit. Formerly they gave out, that all decisions of a Council were, without exception, divine responses. Now, God has extorted this confession from them as if they had been malefactors on the wheel. Whether the Spirit of God presided over the Council must be decided by this test — Did they condemn their own and their fathers' abominations, and turn to true repentance? Let any one who would not be voluntarily deceived try the following canons by this rule. If I do not make it clearer than day that there was not a whir more of repentance in them than in the worst of the Israelites, let it be, as they insist, that it was the voice of God, and not of man. Therefore, as they choose to compare their crew with Ezra, Nehemiah, and the other leaders of the ancient people, and say, by the mouth of their reader, that in the spirit of sorrow they duly lamented their own sins and those of the people, let them, I say, be forgiven for their insolence in putting an atrocious affront on the holy servants of God, by comparing them to a filthy herd of swine, and let them with dry eyes impudently boast of their tears; for what is it that they may not do? Still they cannot deprive us of the liberty of forming our decision from facts rather than words. Herein, indeed, they are very ridiculous. After declaring that they have abundantly wept over their sins in godly sorrow, they exhort themselves and others to open fountains of tears. The rhetorician must surely have been oblivious when he composed this declaration for them: or what if he wished to expose them to derision, as they deserved? The latter may be the true explanation, but I pass it as a matter with which I have no concern.

It were irksome to follow out every single point, nor is it necessary; for they so mingle praise and exhortation, that there is nothing in either but fiction and sheer falsehood. When they accuse our churches of expelling their pastors, substituting laymen in their stead, confounding orders, plundering ecclesiastical property, impeding the course of the word of God, our answer to their accusations is at hand. First, they give the name of pastors to those of whose expulsion they complain, How long will this title be usurped by men who have nothing pastoral but the badge of a silver staff? The confounding of orders which they deplore is nothing else than a moderate restoration of discipline. They insist that they themselves shall be counted sacred in consequence of having been anointed. Fortified with this privilege, they hold that their vices cannot be touched. Hence, provided they may do as they please, everything will be duly ordered. If this sacred order is violated, all things are in their judgment as much confounded as if the heavens were falling. As to the plundering of property, I wish our people were as well prepared to give satisfaction to God as we are to make a candid and true defense against our accusers. That idle-bellies have been deprived of the means which they were swallowing up, I admit. Let us see whether anything was taken by robbery from the Church. It is certain that that which the venerable Legates now dedicate to the Church had been seized by robbers. It is certain that it was not only spent in stuffing their gullet, but basely squandered on debauchery, gaming, theatrical indecencies, and in other ways not a whit better. The poor were neglected. They more frequently squeezed something out of the teachers of schools than aided them with salaries. Now, on the other hand, if the administration is not yet so pure and holy as were to be wished, at least godly pastors are maintained to feed souls with the doctrine of salvation; something is expended on schools; the poor have ten times more distributed to them than they used to get. Some portion also is bestowed on other uses, neither profane nor liable to censure. See why they charge our adherents with plunder! But what have I to say to the charge of impeding the course of the word of God? It is a very serious charge. I am altogether at a loss how to meet it. Nefarious extinguishers of pure doctrine! dare you impute to us the very sacrilege of which you are guilty before God and his angels and the whole world? Yet I wonder not that they spoke so in such a meeting — a meeting to which they knew nothing would be palatable but what was villanously said.

But there were other monitors whose business it was to correct any omission or error of the Legates. There are extant some speeches delivered by monks who, we are to believe, were a kind of channels through which the Holy Spirit flowed out of the mouths of the fathers. There is also one by a bishop, I know not who, than which nothing can be imagined more absurd. The sum of the whole is, that we are to be put down by brief decisions, because it must remain a settled point, that before our friends appeared everything in their doctrine was good and pure. Because Isaiah promises that the Lord will be a wall and rampart to Jerusalem, one Sotus (which in French means stupid and fatuous) devises a twofold bulwark for the Church — one of divine, and another of human laws; and in this foolish imagination he exults as if he were heading a magnificent triumph over us. Could I lose labor and time in hunting down such a creature? To me it is more than enough to have pointed to it with the finger. Because cities are fortified with a wall and rampart, the Lord declares that he alone will serve for both. But the interpretation of Sotus transfers the rampart to human laws, and teaches that the ruins of the Church cannot be restored in any other way than by filling up the breach which we have made.

Another, named Marinarius, exhales smoke from his Carmelite kitchen, and says that our gospel liberty is a pretext for all kinds of corruption; and to give his oration a sprinkling of elegance, he exclaims, — O, impure and vile! Although they have no shame, they will not dare to deny that vice stalks among them with greater freedom than with us. That with us, assuredly, there is more real and chaste severity and a stricter discipline, our daily sermons testify; and yet this dog, just emerged from the mire of a fetid cloister, is not ashamed thus to bark at us. But, after abolishing vows, throwing off celibacy, contemning holy prayers, treading fasting under our feet, and rejecting the customs of our fathers, we have seized on the opportunity of sinning as the leading principle of our life! What kind of life, then, did the Apostles lead? They knew nothing of the celibacy for which the Papists contend; under them there was no mention of vows; they laid no burden on the conscience as to the choice of meats. Contented with the rule which their Lord had prescribed, they attempted not to fetter any by laws and traditions. There is nothing of which we are calumniously accused which might not be equally charged against the Apostles. The kind of vows of which we disapprove is evident from our writings. Into what a sink of impurity the whole world has been plunged by their celibacy, which we desire to change for holy marriage, is but too well known. When Paul censured celibacy in younger widows, his reason was because some of them had gone over to Satan. At the present day it is well ascertained that there is more obscenity in the cloisters of monks and nuns than in common dens of infamy. Wherever priests penetrate they leave some impress of their unchastity; as if they had been prohibited from marriage solely for the purpose of giving free scope to their lust in any quarter. And shall all this experience not have the effect of inducing us to relieve them from the necessity of celibacy? He falsely asserts that we condemn Christian fasting and holy prayer; but he does it securely, because he knew that he would receive the more applause the more bacchanalian rage he vented against us. Meanwhile, this worthy vindicator of gospel liberty describes all the servile superstitions of the papacy as its proper fruits, solace, delight, and nourishment! It is strange he did not also call them celestial nectar and ambrosia! What can you make of an animal like this? Paul teaches that Christian liberty consists in the free use of things indifferent; and though, as is becoming, he makes the external use subordinate to charity, he allows no fetters to be laid on the conscience, and carefully admonishes us to beware of being entangled with the yoke of bondage. This gentle son of Venus (for both his names smack of the sea) affirms that liberty will not be safe unless it be buried under an infinite load of laws and ceremonies; and at length exclaims, that we execrate the approved sayings of the fathers, the sacraments, the honor due to saints, and all that is sacred. By these fictions Papists were formerly wont to stir up the blinded populace against us. Now, it is easy to infer what opinion they have of each other, when this illiberal license of lying catches applause in their most sacred convention.

In what respect, pray, do we impair the honor of the saints, unless it be in forbidding idols to be made of them? Is it honor to the saints to rob God of his honor and transfer it to them, that they may be worshipped promiscuously with God? They will deny that they do so, by bringing in their distinction of *dulia* and *latria*. An excellent method, forsooth, of avoiding idolatry when they distinguish between kinds of worship altogether similar by employing two vocables, just as horses in a stall are kept separate by their tethers. Meanwhile, they allow the saints to be worshipped indifferently with God. What is it that the prophets everywhere condemn in the people of Israel, but just that they give incense to their idols, provide sacred feasts, pay gifts, dedicate altars, and prostrate themselves before them? In all these things the Papists go beyond the Israelites. For they kindle lamps and tapers at the dead images of the dead, sprinkle incense, celebrate their memory in solemn feasts, place them on altars, make oblations to them, carry them about on their shoulders in procession, undertake long pilgrimages to visit them, bow down before them and pray to them. Nay, illiterate females and almost all the peasantry, in praying to Hugo and Lubin, use the very form of prayer which was given us by the Son of God. Thus a block of wood will be our Father in heaven. So far is any one from opposing this horrid sacrilege, that priests and monks sing out, Well done! Well done! And it is made a serious charge against us that we have studied to purify the holy worship of God from all these profanations. Hence we are styled enemies of all that is sacred! And yet no new thing has happened to us; for the same was said of the Prophets and Apostles.

I say nothing of those charges which will be better discussed in their own place. Only there is one which ought not to be omitted, viz., that all we aim at is under the pretext of the primitive and apostolic Church, to set up the carnal daughter of old Adam and the spouse of Satan, instead of a pious Reformation, is to introduce confusion into the Christian commonwealth, and procure license for all kinds of vice; and to leave us no defense, he adds, that all this has been proved by the event. What kind of Church we long for, God well knows and is our witness, while numerous proofs bear ample testimony to the world. A judgment cannot be more truly or rightly formed than from our doctrine and the case itself. Let any one, who will, compare our writings with theirs, and then let him turn his eye and survey the reality. I say nothing more than that it will at once be plain how just our grounds are for bewailing the destruction of the Church, and calling for the restitution of its fallen state; and how in prescribing the method we mingle nothing of carnal prudence or zeal, but refer all our feelings, counsels, wishes, and endeavors to the true and only rule. What agreement or affinity is there between their whole hierarchy which they proudly extol, and the government of Christ and the Apostles? Nay, in what point are they not utterly opposed to each other? But we must pardon Marinarius, who, while he beholds the faces of the Fathers of Trent, is ravished with admiration at the splendid sight, and thinks he sees and hears Christ. Hence, it is not strange that the man in his ecstasy sends forth torrents of froth instead of words! He says: While I contemplate you, Fathers, pre-eminent in ecclesiastical dignity, and distinguished for all kinds of learning, you the lights and ornaments of the world, methinks I see Christ walking on the water, and also hear him saying, Fear not: it is I! The reason why he inveighs so fiercely against us is because we set no more value on that divine splendor of the Council of Trent, at which he gazes in amazement, than on a children's show. In what terms shall I rebuke his sordid adulation? But anything from a Carmelite scarcely deserves rebuke, since the world has long been accustomed not to require anything like ingenuousness in that begging fraternity.

Next, Ambrosius Catharinus, of the order of the Dominicans, the old antagonist of Luther, blows out his cheeks. I thought that under

the confusion to which he was put twenty years ago, he had gone into
some obscure corner to hide himself. So disgracefully was he prostrated
by Luther, when yet a young soldier, so thoroughly was he hissed by the
consent of all classes, that if he were wise he would never have appeared
again in public. But now, I presume, aroused by the published bull of
the Council, as if a jubilee had been proclaimed, he again comes to
light a kind of new man. He is the same, however, as before. Those
who formerly read the absurdities of Catharinus would not know that
that putrid carcass is still breathing, did they not read his harangues
delivered in the Council, in which the mother of Christ is called his
most faithful associate, and represented as sitting on his throne to obtain
grace for us! Many before him have given loose reins to their impudence,
but none I believe was found, while seeking to deck the blessed Virgin
with fictitious titles, to call her the associate of Christ. And that this
blasphemous expression was uttered in such an assembly, and received
with no small favor, posterity never would have believed had not the
oration been published. What is meant by dividing Christ, if this is not?
Therefore, when he says that she has been appointed by God to be our
advocate, it is just equivalent to saying that half of what the Apostles
declare of Christ is applicable to her. And this fellow dares to compare
himself to Simeon, though the venerable old man had his whole soul
intent on the one salvation of God, even not yet revealed, whereas to
Catharinus Christ is only one among a crowd of advocates. After making this beautiful arrangement in heaven, he descends to the terrestrial
hierarchy, and declares that whoso refuses to submit to Paul 3 is an alien
from the body of Christ! What! even though he hold a primacy only like
that of the devil among his angels?

He says, that he who holds the See of Rome cannot but be the Vicar
of Christ. Are these triflers not yet ashamed to sport their futile inanities,

which they know to have been refuted a thousand times to weariness? At the period when there was still a Church and a bishopric at Rome, there was no mention of any such primacy as the Romanists now arrogate to themselves. To Christ alone belongs the universal bishopric, while each single pastor, as Cyprian tells us, possesses part of the undivided whole. The appellation of Universal Bishop, if conferred on a man, Gregory everywhere testifies to be blasphemous, nefarious, accursed, and the forerunner of Antichrist. What! were the Africans cut off from the body of Christ when they would not even concede the title of first or highest bishop to the bishop of Rome? Did Cyprian discard himself from the communion of the Church, when he not only called Stephen the Roman bishop to order, and taught him to be docile to his colleagues, but charged him with error, ignorance, and mulish obstinacy? Was Jerome the author of schism from the flock of Christ, when he declared that no bishop was made superior by the pride of riches, nor inferior by the humility of poverty, — whether he were the bishop of Rome or of Eugubium? But though with one assent the Roman See were raised to the third heaven, how ridiculous is it to make a primate of bishops of one who is no more like a bishop than a wolf is like a lamb! It is little to say that there is nothing episcopal in him, but while he is the declared enemy of Christ and the Church, it is surely too much to insist on our acknowledging him to be also The Vicar of Christ? At present, however, it is not our purpose to carry this discussion farther. It is better to consult our books on this subject. The words of Catharinus himself remind us that we must not stay longer here. For after swearing that the last thing he would do would be to curry favor by flattery, he immediately adds, — "But to the subject," — intimating that he had wandered and spoken away from the subject. It is hopeless, however, to expect that he will bring us back to the subject, unless he previously return to a sound mind.

If we may judge a lion by his claws, our readers now have the means of knowing what they ought to think of the Council of Trent. For it is to be supposed, that of the monks present, those to whom chiefly the task of discoursing was given, were deemed the first and as it were the flower. Let it be understood that they are also the persons who concocted the Canons, and dictated to the horned Fathers what they, like dumb persons, were to approve by a silent nod. To what have we fallen! Are we to give the honor of Divine oracles to whatever such creatures might growl with obstreperous voice into other ears? Although I am not so ignorant of matters as to believe that the orations published in their name, be they what they may, were their own composition; for they have their speechmakers, to whom they hand their absurdities, and get them glossed over with some color of words, lest even children should laugh! But let us assume that the whole was polished by their own industry, still it is a great point gained to have such a specimen of the awful wisdom of the Papacy.

We must not pass over some bishop or other named Cornelius, who, as he surpassed his superiors in dignity, far surpasses them also in folly. Had there been anything like gravity and seriousness in the Acts of the Council, one might have said that the part assigned to him was that of the fool in the play; but there is no doubt that he was a chosen one among the bishops, though the whole flower of the order was displayed; and therefore I only say, that if they were not sorry for him and ashamed of him, I very much pity them. Their eyes indeed may have been dazzled by one circumstance — his gathering flowers from every quarter, and thrusting into his oration every elegant expression he had ever learnt, that he might pass himself off as an orator. And I for one am perfectly willing that he should think himself most eloquent, and seem so to his party. He must, indeed, have been very familiar with Cicero, from whom he with so much confidence borrows patches of sentences, which he huddles into his discourse. But that, while thus playing the buffoon, he should employ his borrowed garrulity to oppress the kingdom of Christ and profane Scripture at will, is not on any account to be borne. It were an endless work to specify every point, but the reader may take the following as a specimen. The joyous orator, after pouring upon his audience his three-fold joy, congratulates himself and his associates that they now see with their eyes and handle with their hands that blessed hope which many desired to see but were not able. These words once spoken, partly of the former advent of Christ, and partly of the final revelation for which we still look, what pious man can, without indignation, hear transferred by this madman to such a sink as Trent? And that nothing might be wanting to crown his impudence, he tags to it a third clause from the eleventh chapter of Hebrews, on the final perfection of believers.

After this prelude, what might he not think himself at liberty to do? Accordingly, he hesitates not to strip Christ in order that he may deck his Pope with the spoils. The Pope, he says, came a light into the world. Blasphemous mouth! will you apply to that fetid monster of yours sacred terms applicable to none but the Son of God? Had you believed in a God, must not the very sound of your nefarious voice have struck you with sudden horror and amazement? Had there been any feeling of piety in that famous Council, must not this great profanation of Scripture, and more especially this insult to the Son of God, have inflamed all with indignation? And will they still pretend that the Holy Spirit presides where our Redeemer is with such impunity mocked? For what is more peculiar to Christ than the honor which the evangelist renders to him when, excluding the Baptist by name, or rather under his name excluding all mortals, he asserts of Christ alone, and proclaims that the Son of God came as our light from heaven? It is one of those sentences which must produce the highest reverence in all pious minds. The Council, however, receive it as if it were mere gaudy verbiage. What words of rebuke could be strong enough for such impiety? But it is well that my readers have no need of many words to form a just estimate of it; for which reason I shall merely glance at the remainder

When he breaks forth in praise of Paul III, one would say that he has drawn his water from a full fountain, there is such a flow of words. He is, he says, the bravest and best in the memory of man; he will be celebrated by the tongues of all nations; no age will be silent in his praise! He had read these things in Cicero. He thought them elegantly expressed — as indeed they are — provided they be aptly applied. How well they apply to Paul 3 let the consciences even of those who are most devoted to his tyranny bear witness. I were more than foolish were I to detail the encomiums in the thundering out of which this trifler exercises his lungs. After saying that he was preserved by the wondrous providence of God to bless us with his faith, wisdom, and power, he bids the venerable Fathers, as sitting on a kind of tripod, exclaim, Long life to the Holiest — Long life to the Ecumenical — Long life to the Apostolical! O good father, how much better were it for you to be a man of sense than to sing out your vivat in favor not only of a dead man, but of a fatal pestiferous monster! As to your proclaiming him worthy of heaven, I don't know if you are aware of the universal belief that he was unworthy of the earth! Here you certainly made a most grievous mistake; you ought to have assigned him a station far removed from heaven. Of the remaining bundle of praises with which this elegant eulogist loads his idol, I will only say this much: He had perhaps heard the old adage, Praise is a pleasant song — but mistook its meaning. Accordingly, that he might show himself a pleasant orator, his whole oration is devoted to praise. He next passes to the Council; and of the three Legates makes one a celestial, viz., Cardinal de Monti, whom all know to be truculent in temper and rude in manners; the second he makes a strict exacter of Christian policy, (I wish he would begin with his own bed-chamber!) and the third he makes an angel, (I wish he would lay aside his ambition, a principal part of the flesh!) At length the Council appears to him like the New Jerusalem, and what not. This no doubt was in compliance with the grave obtestation of the Legates, that no man should be praised. But the amusing part is, that though he intended to say all these things, he deprecates their indignation. Let none of you, he says, be offended with me; for better are the wounds of a friend than the treacherous kisses of an enemy. They must surely be cruel, ravenous beasts if such soft handling irritates them. What would they do under harder provocation?

Afterwards, as if he had appeased them, he gives way to exultation, exclaiming, We came, and saw, and conquered! Caesar indeed might thus boast. But how ridiculous are these paeans in the shade of the valley of Trent, out of sight of an enemy! I should like to know what they saw to conquer? But I am afraid he may charge me with misrepresenting; since he immediately adds the reason, viz., that the gates of the Council being opened, the gates of heaven were opened also, as if it were not palpable to all how wide the difference is between heaven and the Council. But we must pardon a delirious man when he wanders out of bounds. He next congratulates them on the restoration of the Church, which was nodding to destruction, when the new light of God, and of him who makes the nearest approach to God — Paul 3 — arose! What! is Paul 3 superior to angels, and Prophets, and Apostles? I see how it is. He had read that Cicero (whom he imitates not quite so well as a monkey does a man) had on one occasion thus flattered the Roman people, and he was unwilling to lose the fine sentence. Meanwhile, what pious mind does not abominate such blasphemy.

Who can say that the Spirit was absent from a Council which was blown up by such bellows? And yet this bishopling does make a glowing harangue about the clemency of Paul III and the Fathers. For he declares that Paul, forgetful of himself, and mindful of us, aimed solely at what was humane and fatherly. We will believe that the mind of Paul was thus mild, whenever it shall appear that he forgot himself. This coloring, however, is far more tolerable than the cruel instigation of a rhetorician, I say not who, (for from respect I suppress his name.) Afraid, perhaps, that the men of Trent would not be bold enough in issuing sanguinary decrees, he exhorts them to dare, and promises that the moment they order, hands will be ready to execute. Is it thus that you, who are not ignorant of their disposition, and ought rather, if conscience had any weight with you, to have exposed your own head — is it thus that to subject the innocent to unworthy treatment, you hesitate not to whet the fury of men already possessed by cruel and brutish rage? Has the Italian air so debased all your feelings, as to make you forget that the Son of God, whose cause is discussed, will one day be a just Judge? Have you forgotten how great value he sets upon his kingdom, which is comprehended under the preaching of the Word? Do you not hear in mind how strict an avenger he declares himself to be, when his Father's glory is infringed? By what figures of rhetoric will you efface the fearful judgments which he fulminates against perfidious dissimulation? What madness has so blinded you, that you fear not to trample under foot the sacred blood of martyrs, which he declares, and not in vain declares, to be precious in his sight? Does not this single sentence strike you with terror, — Woe to those who call light darkness? I tremble on your account, while I think of that fearful vengeance which must shortly overtake you, if you return not to the right path. I therefore spare you not, in order that God may spare. But so it, is. The tongues of rhetoricians must become meretricious when they begin to speak for hire. But if they are so eloquent in cursing, we must not be dumb in repressing their virulence. It were base cowardice if, while they pour all possible opprobrium on the memory of the martyrs, (which the Lord hath with his own lips declared would be blessed among the righteous,) we should tamely allow it; it were flagitious perfidy if, while they defame the eternal truth of God, we should in a manner betray it by our silence! But let us now come to the decree of the Second Session, as the first act of the play.

DECREE PUBLISHED IN THE SECOND SESSION OF THE HOLY COUNCIL OF TRENT.

7 TH JANUARY 1546.

The Holy Council of Trent lawfully met in the Holy Spirit, under the presidency of the three foresaid Legates of the Apostolic See, acknowledging, with the blessed Apostle James, that every good and perfect gift is from above, coming down from the Father of Lights, who to all who ask wisdom of him, giveth liberally, and upbraideth not; and knowing, also, that the fear of the Lord is the beginning of wisdom, hath determined and decreed that all and each of the faithful in Christ, assembled in the city of Trent, are to be exhorted, as the Council hereby exhorts them, to turn aside from the evil and sins they have hitherto committed, and walk henceforth in the fear of the Lord, and not fulfill the desires of the flesh; to be instant in prayer, frequent in confession, take the sacrament of the Eucharist, attend the churches, in short, accomplish the commandments of the Lord, (as far as each may be enabled,) and likewise pray in private every day for the peace of Christian rulers, and the unity of the Church; that Bishops, moreover, and all others in priests' orders, assisting at the (Ecumenical Council in this city, make it their business to engage diligently in the praises of the Lord, offering victims, praises, and prayers, and perform the sacrifice of the Mass, at least every Lord's Day, (on which God made the light, and rose again from the dead, and imparted the Holy Spirit to his disciples,) offering up, as the Holy Spirit enjoins by the Apostle, supplications, prayers, requests, and thanksgivings, for our most holy lord the Pope, for the Emperor, for kings, and others who are in authority, and for all men, that we may lead a quiet and tranquil life, enjoy peace, and see an increase of faith. The Council, moreover, exhorts them to fast, at least every Friday, in memory of our Lord's passion, and bestow alms on the poor. Moreover, in the cathedral church, let there be a Mass of the Holy Spirit celebrated every Thursday, with the litanies and other prayers thereunto appointed; and in the other churches, on the same day, let at least litanies and prayers be said. And during the time of Divine service, let there be no speaking and gossiping, but let the minister be accompanied with mouth and mind.

And seeing that bishops must be blameless, sober, chaste, ruling their own houses well, the Council also exhorts every one above all things to observe sobriety and moderation at table; and as there idle talk usually begins, to have the Holy Scriptures read at their tables, each teaching and training those of his household, not to be quarrelsome, drunken, unchaste, covetous, heady, slanderous, and lovers of pleasures, in short, to shun vice, and embrace virtue; and as regards dress and behavior, let them study comeliness in all their actions, as befit the ministers of God.

Moreover, seeing that the principal care, solicitude, and aim of this Holy Council is to drive away the darkness of the heresies which have for so many years covered the land, and with the aid of Jesus Christ, who is the true light, to make the light of Catholic truth shine again in all its brightness and purity, and to reform those things which need reformation, the Council exhorts all Catholics here met and to meet, and especially those skilled in sacred literature, to consider diligently with themselves by what ways and means the intention of the Council may be directed, so as best to obtain the wished for result, that thus things worthy of condemnation may be more quickly and advisedly condemned, and those worthy of approval approved, and all men throughout the world may with one voice and the same confession of faith glorify God and the Father of our Lord Jesus Christ.

And while the priests sitting in the place of benediction give their opinions, agreeably to the Canon of the Council of Toulouse, let none use immoderate expressions, or act tumultuously, let none contend with false, vain, or obstinate disputation, but let all be said in the mildest terms, that neither may the hearers be offended, nor the edge of judgment be blunted by perturbation of mind.

Moreover, the Sacred Council has resolved and decreed, that if it shall happen that any sit in a place not duly belonging to them, and give their vote by using the word placet, and take part in the meetings, and do any other acts whatsoever during the Council, none shall thereby suffer prejudice, none acquire new rights.

ON THE DECREE OF THE SECOND SESSION.

A s they know that the name of Council is held in honor, they use it for the purpose of procuring respect to themselves from good men, to whom they are unknown; for while they keep using such swelling words as Sacred, Ecumenical, and Universal Council, lawfully met in the Holy Spirit, they dazzle the eyes of the simple. But as it is a part of Christian modesty to reverence the authority of the Church, so it is the part of prudence to take heed that Satan do not delude us by a fallacious pretext. Here, indeed, there is no necessity for such careful prudence; for we have not to guard against spiritual imposture, or some more hidden subtlety. Let us only open our eyes, and we shall see that what they clothe in such splendid titles is nothing. When they published this Canon, perhaps twenty bishops were present. This is what they call an Universal Council, and the more to overawe the ignorant, they use a Greek term, as if an unknown word were to have the power of a magical charm! But what is meant by calling it an OEcumenical Council? It is the same as if it were said that all the bishops throughout the habitable globe had flocked to Trent. Had it been only a Provincial Council they should have been ashamed of the fewness of its members. Why, then, or on what ground shall we regard this as a Holy Council? How long, pray, will they think that they are dealing with children, and can add to their dignity by pomposities fit only to excite laughter? How can they make us believe that they are duly met in the Holy Spirit, unless it be that they were summoned by bull? As if they held men's minds fascinated by the absurd idea, that the Holy Spirit is brought down from heaven by the nod of a Pope. At the time when those Councils were held, to which they themselves are obliged to give preeminence, the Roman bishop did not possess the right of calling them. The Emperor, along with others, summoned them by his edict. That this was the case not only with what are called the four great Councils, but also with very many others, is attested by ancient acts still extant, and by all history. Let them not here allege that the validity of such summoning was questionable. This is disproved by the letters of Leo, in which he humbly begs the Emperors Theodosius, Valentinian, and Marcion, that they would be pleased, of their imperial authority, to intimate a day and place for the bishops. Gregory long after begged the same of Mauricius.

But, perhaps, the three Legates of the Apostolic See brought the Holy Spirit. If so, the Council of Nice was not duly assembled, since it only gave the Legates of the Roman Church the fourth place. What is to be said of the Council of Aquila, which, though it was held in Italy, and was a general Council, makes no mention of the Roman bishop? If a Council is not duly constituted unless the Legates of the Pope preside, what answer will the African bishops give who assigned the last place to Philip and Asellus, the two Legates of Boniface, because they were only presbyters and not of the episcopal order? Now, if a deacon of the

Roman Church is only distinguished by a red cloak, he will carry his head over those of all the bishops. However, it is of no consequence to me what rank each of them holds. I will give them no trouble on that head. Nay, I will readily allow the mitres to be vanquished by the hats, provided they do not bind the Holy Spirit to their masks of recent invention, and maintain, that wherever the purple glare is seen, the Council is duly assembled. But if they lay down this as the law, why do they refuse to hold the Council at Basle to have been a lawful Council? Who can tolerate the insolent pretense, that a man can send forth the Spirit and recall him when he pleases? If they would convince us by a sound argument that the Spirit of God is their President, they must first prove that they are assembled in the name and under the auspices of Christ.

Their acts proclaim that it is far otherwise. First, their lofty preamble is not followed up by anything worthy of the occasion; and, secondly, as soon as they enter upon business, the very best they have is drawn from the veriest dregs of superstition. At the very commencement, how flat and lifeless they are, and devoid of all spiritual energy in their first Canon, I will leave to the judgment of my readers. There is no man possessed of moderate intelligence who does not see this for himself. It is sufficient to touch on what follows. One simple fact will enable us to give judgment. They exhort the bishops and priests holding the Council, in other words, themselves, to perform the sacrifice of the Mass at least every Lord's day. Behold the beginning of their famous Reformation! We loudly maintain that the sacrifice of the Mass is nothing else than an impious profanation of the Lord's Supper. This we make plain by the clear words of our Lord. For in instituting the sacred Supper, he does not enjoin us to sacrifice, but invites us to partake of the sacrifice which he himself once offered. He commands distribution to be made, and orders all alike to communicate in both symbols. And there is no obscurity in the words; Take, distribute among yourselves; drink ye all of this cup. What resemblance is there between the observance which corresponds to our Lord's command and the Papal Mass, in which they pretend that Christ offers himself to the Father to expiate the sins of the world by the sacrifice of himself, and not only so, but also to obtain redemption for the dead — in which no invitation is given to partake, but one individual sets himself apart from the whole flock — and where, if any one comes forward to partake, the half is withheld from him?

Anciently, when the people were remiss in their attendance, Chrysostom said, In vain stand we at the altar. He said this at a time when he had been used to many corruptions. What will our Lord say when his ordinance is not only corrupted but altogether subverted? Let them go then, and anew, by their sacrilege, provoke the anger of the Lord, already too much awakened. Next, they exhort all to fast every Friday in remembrance of our Lord's passion, etc. Is this what Paul teaches concerning the observance of days? Is this his admonition regarding the choice of meats, in the same Epistle, where he calls it eqeloqrhskeia (ἐθελοθρησκεία), i.e., a factitious worship, which, however it may have a show of wisdom, being founded only on the decisions of men, vanishes along with the meats which perish in the using? Where, pray, have they read that the Lord commanded such a commemoration of his death? Nay, rather by his death, everything of the kind was abolished. What then is to be said of those preparatory steps by which they wish to bring the Holy Spirit down from heaven? What, but just that they are fatuous superstitions fit for old women to talk of when sitting with the wool and distaff. To these they add litanies, that is, chants consisting of as many blasphemies as words. With what gloss will they excuse their passing by the intercession of Christ in perfect silence, and choosing hundreds of advocates for themselves at will from among the dead? What resemblance has the doctrine of Scripture, or the primitive customs of the godly, to their conduct in omitting the one Mediator of God and man, fixing by name or mediations which they have assumed at their own hand, and at length invoking the whole body of the saints, as if they were all bound up in one bundle? However they permit themselves to depart from the pure doctrine of the Gospel, it is certain that at a time when superstition had so far prevailed, that holy pastors could not hold the straight course, it was prohibited in distinct terms by the Council of Carthage, to invoke saints at the altar, or the priest was forbidden to use the expression, "St. Peter or St. Paul, pray for us." What reformation is to be hoped from those whose degeneracy so much outstrips even a degenerate eye?

FIRST DECREE PUBLISHED IN THE THIRD SESSION OF THE COUNCIL OF TRENT.

THURSDAY, FEBRUARY 4, 1546.

In the Name of the Holy and undivided Trinity, Father, Son, and Holy Spirit. This Sacred, Ecumenical, and General Council of Trent, lawfully met in the Holy Spirit, under the presidency of the foresaid three Legates of the Apostolic See, considering the magnitude of the affairs to be handled, especially those which are included under the two heads of Extirpating Heresies and Reforming Manners, for which purposes especially it has met; and acknowledging with the Apostle that

it has to wrestle not only with flesh and blood, but with spiritual wickednesses in high places, with the same Apostle, specially exhorts all and each
to be strong in the Lord and in the power of his might, in all things taking
the shield of faith whereby they may be able to ward off all the fiery darts
of the wicked one, and receive the helmet of the hope of salvation, which
is the word of God. Wherefore, that this pious solicitude of the Council
may have its beginning and progress by the grace of God, it has before
all things determined and decreed to prefix a Confession of Faith, herein
following the examples of the Fathers, who in more solemn Councils
were wont to set up this shield against all heresies at the commencement
of their proceedings; by which alone they sometimes drew over infidels
to the faith, routed heretics, and confirmed the faithful. That Creed,
therefore, which the Holy Roman Church uses as the first principles in
which all who profess the Christian faith necessarily agree, and the firm
and only foundation against which the gates of hell shall never prevail,
the Council has judged it proper to express in the very words in which it
is read in the churches, and which is as follows: —

"I believe in one God the Father Almighty, Maker of heaven and earth,
of all things visible and invisible: And in our Lord Jesus Christ, the
only-begotten Son of God, and born of the Father before all ages: God
of God, light of light, very God of very God, begotten not made, of one
substance with the Father, by whom all things were made: Who because
of us men and our salvation came down from the heavens, and was
incarnate of the Holy Spirit by the Virgin Mary; and became man: He
was also crucified for us under Pontius Pilate, suffered and was buried,
and rose again on the third day, according to the Scriptures, and ascended
into heaven, and sitteth on the right hand of the Father: And he will come
again with glory to judge the quick and the dead; and of his kingdom
there will be no end. And I believe in the Holy Spirit, the Lord and giver

of life, who proceedeth from the Father and the Son, who with the Father and the Son is worshipped and glorified; who spake by the Prophets. And I believe in one Holy Catholic and Apostolic Church. I acknowledge one baptism for the remission of sins, and I wait for the resurrection of the dead and the life of the world to come. Amen."

Moreover, the Holy, (Ecumenical, and General Council of Trent, lawfully met in the Holy Spirit, under the presidency of the foresaid three Legates of the Apostolic See, understanding that many prelates from different quarters are prepared for the journey, and some also are on their way, and considering that all the things to be decreed by the Holy Council may seem to be in higher estimation and honor with all, the greater and fuller the Council and attendance of Fathers by which they are sanctioned and confirmed, the Council have determined and decreed that the next Session after the present will be held on the first Thursday following the Laetare Sunday next to come. Meanwhile, however, they will take care that the discussion and examination of the matters which may seem proper to be discussed and examined by the Council be not deferred.

ON THE DECREE OF THE THIRD SESSION.

O ne might think that the venerable Fathers mean something very lofty when they talk of the spiritual armor of St. Paul. But from the swollen mountain nothing but empty smoke comes forth, nothing at least that can be of any use in our present necessity; for they only subscribe the Confession of Faith which is chanted in churches. They had published a decree in the beginning of January; they delay the publication of this second one till February. What need was there of such long deliberation in a clear matter? Was this the result of a month's investigation? They must be very diligent and laborious in difficult matters, if they are so long occupied when they have nothing to do. Therefore, that they might not appear to have spent time to no purpose, when the day arrives, — "the leaders seated and the vulgar thronged around," — they with loud voice proclaim their belief in points as to which all men knew there was no dispute. They will say that they did so according to form and custom. But did a ceremonial of no difficulty require a whole month? This device, while they sit saying nothing, is certainly too puerile to prove that they have not been idle. But with what gravity do they pronounce? They say we profess to believe the Creed as it is in the Missal. Though I were not to expose their trifling, it is strange that they are not themselves ashamed of it. As to the many prelates whom they supposed on the way to them from various quarters, they were in a mistake. For at last scarcely forty were collected. They therefore lost the high estimation which they expected from their great numbers. And yet, in my opinion, they do themselves injustice when they make fewness of numbers a disparagement. So high is their authority with me, that five hundred men like themselves would not give the least additional weight to it!

Chapter 5

FIRST DECREE OF THE FOURTH SESSION OF THE COUNCIL OF TRENT.

H ELD 8TH APRIL 1546.

THE Holy, Ecumenical, and General Council of Trent, lawfully met in the Holy Spirit, under the presidency of the foresaid three Legates of the Apostolic See, keeping it constantly in view that by the removal of error the full purity of the Gospel may be preserved in the Church; which Gospel promised before by the prophets, our Lord Jesus Christ the Son of God first promulgated with his own lips, and afterwards ordered to be published by his Apostles to every creature, as the fountain of all saving truth and moral discipline; and perceiving

that this truth and discipline is contained in written books, and unwritten traditions which, received from the lips of Christ himself by
the Apostles, or as it were handed down by the Apostles themselves
under the inspiration of the Holy Spirit, have come even to us —
following the example of orthodox Fathers, the Council with like
pious affection and reverence receives and venerates all the Books both
of the Old and New Testaments, seeing that one God is the author of
both — and likewise also the traditions pertaining both to faith and
manners, as dictated either by the lips of Christ or by the Holy Spirit,
and preserved by uninterrupted succession in the Catholic Church.
It has been thought proper to subjoin a list of the Sacred Books to
this Decree, that no doubt may arise as to what the Books are which
the Council receives. They are as, follows: Of the Old Testament the
Five Books of Moses, i.e., Genesis, Exodus, Leviticus, Numbers, and
Deuteronomy; Joshua, Judges, Ruth; four Books of Kings; two of
Chronicles; the first Book of Esdras, and the second, which is called
Nehemiah; Tobit, Judith, Hester, Job; the Psalter of David, con-
taining one hundred and fifty Psalms; the Proverbs, Ecclesiastes, the
Song of Songs, the Book of Wisdom, Ecclesiasticus; Isaiah, Jeremiah,
with Baruch, Ezekiel, Daniel; the twelve Minor Prophets, i.e., Hosea,
Joel, Amos, Abdias, Jonah, Micah, Nahum, Habakkuk, Zephani-
ah, Haggai, Zachariah, Malachi; two Books of Maccabees, the First
and Second; of the New Testament, the four Gospels according to
Matthew, Mark, Luke, and John; the Acts of the Apostles, written by
the Evangelist Luke; fourteen Epistles of the Apostle Paul, viz., to the
Romans, two to the Corinthians, to the Galatians, to the Ephesians,
to the Philippians, to the Colossians, two to the Thessalonians, two to
Timothy, to Titus, to Philemon, to the Hebrews; two of the Apostle
Peter; three of the Apostle John; one of the Apostle James; one of the
Apostle Jude, and the Apocalypse of the Apostle John. Whosoever

shall not receive these entire Books, with all their parts, as they are accustomed to be read in the Catholic Church, and are contained in the old Vulgate Latin edition, as sacred and canonical, and shall knowingly and intentionally despise the foresaid traditions, let him be anathema. Wherefore, let all understand the way and order in which the Council, after laying the foundation of a Confession of Faith is to proceed, and what testimonies and. supports it will chiefly employ in confirming doctrines and renewing discipline in the Church.

SECOND DECREE OF THE FOURTH SESSION.

M oreover, the foresaid Holy Council considering that it may confer no small benefit on the Church of God, if from among
all the Latin editions of the Sacred Books which are in use, it notifies
what one is to be held authentic, it statutes and declares that the ancient
Vulgate edition, approved by its long use for so many centuries in the
Church itself, be held authentic in public lectures, debates, sermons, and
expositions; and that no man is to dare or presume on any pretext to
reject it.

Besides, in order to curb petulant minds, the Council decrees that
no man trusting to his own wisdom, in matters of faith and discipline
pertaining to the edification of Christian doctrine, twisting the Sacred
Scripture to his own sense, dare to interpret the Holy Scripture contrary
to that sense which holy mother Church, to whom it belongs to judge

of the true sense and interpretation of the Holy Scriptures, has held and holds, or even contrary to the unanimous consent of the Fathers, even though these interpretations are never to be published. Let those who contravene be denounced by the ordinaries, and punished with the pains appointed by law.

Wishing, also, as is proper, to regulate printers in this matter, who now, without regulation, i.e., thinking themselves at liberty to act as they please, without license from their ecclesiastical superiors, print the books of Holy Scripture, and, moreover, annotations and expositions of whatever description, often without mentioning the press, or giving a fictitious one, and (what is worse) without the author's name, and have books of this description printed elsewhere promiscuously for sale; the Council statutes and decrees, that hereafter the Holy Scriptures, and especially the ancient Vulgate edition, be printed as correctly as possible, and that no one be allowed to print, or cause to be printed, any books on sacred subjects without the name of the author, nor in future to sell them, or even have them in his possession, unless they have been first examined and approved by the Ordinary, under pain of anathema, and the penalty mentioned in the canon of the last Lateran Council. If the persons be Regulars, not subject to this mode of examination and approbation, they shall be bound to obtain a license from their superiors, after the books have been recognized by them according to the form of their own ordinances.

Those who lend or circulate these works in manuscript, before they have been examined and approved, shall be liable to the same penalties as the printers; and those who shall have had them, or read them, if they do not. give up the author, shall be held to be authors. The approbation of this class of books must be given in writing, and appear authenticated in front of the book, or manuscript, or print. The whole of this duty, i.e., the examination and approbation, must be done gratuitously, so that what deserves approval may be approved, and disapprobation reprobated.

Moreover, wishing to repress the temerity by which the words of Holy Scripture are turned and twisted to all kinds of profanity — to buffoonery, fable, vanity, adulation, detraction, impious superstitions, diabolical charms, divinations, casting of lots, and also slanderous libels, the Council commands and ordains, in order to put an end to such irreverence and contempt, and prevent any one from daring, in future, in any way to use the words of Scripture for these and similar purposes, that all persons of this description, all corrupters and violators of the Word of God, shall be coerced by their bishops by legal and discretionary punishment.

Likewise the Holy Council has statuted and decreed, that the next session shall be held and celebrated on the fifth day after the most sacred festival of Pentecost ensuing.

ON THE FOURTH SESSION

There is an old proverb, — The Romans conquer by sitting. Trusting to this, those degenerate and bastard sons of the Roman See, i.e., the great harlot, sat down to conquer when they appointed the third session. For what hinders them from raising a trophy, and coming off victorious to their hearts content, if we concede to them what they have comprehended in one decree? There are four heads: First, they ordain that in doctrine we are not to stand on Scripture alone, but also on things handed down by tradition. Secondly, in forming a catalogue of Scripture, they mark all the books with the same chalk, and insist on placing the Apocrypha in the same rank with the others. Thirdly, repudiating all other versions whatsoever, they retain the Vulgate only, and order it to be authentic. Lastly, in all passages either dark or doubtful, they claim the right of interpretation without challenge. These four things being established, who can deny that the war is ended? Wherefore, their after discussions were more for ostentation than from any necessity for them;

for whatever they produce, if supported by no authority of Scripture, will be classed among traditions, which they insist should have the same authority as the Law and the Prophets. What, then, will it be permitted to disapprove? for there is no gross old wife's dream which this pretext will not enable them to defend; nay, there is no superstition, however monstrous, in front of which they may not place it like a shield of Ajax. Add to this, that they provide themselves with new supports when they give full authority to the Apocryphal books. Out of the second of the Maccabees they will prove Purgatory and the worship of saints; out of Tobit satisfactions, exorcisms, and what not. From Ecclesiasticus they will borrow not a little. For from whence could they better draw their dregs? I am not one of those, however, who would entirely disapprove the reading of those books; but in giving them in authority which they never before possessed, what end was sought but just to have the use of spurious paint in coloring their errors? But as the Hebrew or Greek original often serves to expose their ignorance in quoting Scripture, to check their presumption, and so keep down their thrasonic boasting, they ingeniously meet this difficulty also by determining that the Vulgate translation only is to be held authentic. Farewell, then, to those who have spent much time and labor in the study of languages, that they might search for the genuine sense of Scripture at the fountainhead! At least it has been amply provided by this decree that they shall give no farther trouble to the Romanists. Is not this to subdue Greece and all the East? One thing still was wanting; for disagreeable men were always springing up, who, when anything was brought into question, could not be satisfied without Scripture proof! There are others too clear-sighted, since even in the Vulgate translation they find weapons wherewith to annoy the Papacy. That they may not sustain loss from this quarter, they devise a most excellent remedy, when they adjudge to themselves the legitimate interpretation of Scripture. Who can now imagine any improvidence in them? By one article they have obtained the means of proving what they please out of Scripture, and escaping from every passage that might be urged against them. If Confession is to be proved, they are ready with — "Show yourselves to the priests." If it be asked, Whether recourse should be had to the intercession of the dead? the passage will immediately occur, "Turn to some one of the saints;" also, "For this every holy man will pray to thee." Nor will Purgatory be left without a sure foundation, for it is written, "He shall not come out thence till he shall have paid the uttermost farthing." In short, anything may be made of anything! When they formerly produced such passages they made themselves ridiculous even to children. Now, if credit is given them, the right of authorized interpretation will remove every doubt. For what passage can be objected to them so clear and strong that they shall not evade it? Any kind of quibble will at once relieve them from difficulty. Against opposing arguments they will set up this brazen wall — Who are you to question the interpretation of the Church? This, no doubt, is what they mean by a saying common among them, in that Scripture is a nose of wax, because it can be formed into all shapes. If postulates of this kind were given to mathematicians, they would not only make an ell an inch, but prove a mile shorter than an ell, till they had thrown everything into confusion.

What, then, are we to do with this victorious and now, as it were, triumphal Session? Just stand and let the smoke clear away. In regard to Traditions, I am aware that not unfrequent mention of them is made by ancient writers, though not with the intention of carrying our faith beyond the Scriptures, to which they always confine it. They only say that certain customs were received from the Apostles. Some of them appear to have that origin, but others are unworthy of it. These touch only upon a few points, and such as might be tolerated. But now we are called to believe, that whatever the Romanists are pleased to obtrude upon us, flowed by tradition from the Apostles; and so shameless are they, that without observing any distinction, they bring into this class things which crept in not long ago, during the darkness of ignorance. Therefore, though we grant that the Apostles of the Lord handed down to posterity some customs which they never committed to writing; still, first, this has nothing to do with the doctrine of faith, (as to it we cannot extract one iota from them,) but only with external rites subservient to decency or discipline; and secondly, it is still necessary for them to prove that everything to which they give the name is truly an apostolical tradition. Accordingly they cannot, as they suppose, find anything here to countenance them either in establishing the tyranny of their laws, by which they miserably destroy consciences, or to cloak their superstitions, which are evidently a farrago gathered from the vicious rites of all ages and nations. We especially repudiate their desire to make certainty of doctrine depend not less on what they call agrafa, (unwritten,) than on the Scriptures. We must ever adhere to Augustine's rule, "Faith is conceived from the Scriptures."

Of their admitting all the Books promiscuously into the Canon, I say nothing more than it is done against the consent of the primitive Church. It is well known what Jerome states as the common opinion of earlier times. And Ruffinus, speaking of the matter as not at all controverted, declares with Jerome that Ecclesiasticus, the Wisdom of Solomon, Tobit, Judith, and the history of the Maccabees, were called by the Fathers not canonical but ecclesiastical books, which might indeed be read to the people, but were not entitled to establish doctrine. I am not, however, unaware that the same view on which the Fathers of Trent now insist was held in the Council of Carthage. The same, too, was followed by Augustine in his Treatise on Christian Doctrine; but as he testifies that all of his age did not take the same view, let us assume that the point was then undecided. But if it were to be decided by arguments drawn from the case itself, many things beside the phraseology would show that those Books which the Fathers of Trent raise so high must sink to a lower place. Not to mention other things, whoever it was that wrote the history of the Maccabees expresses a wish, at the end, that he may have written well and congruously; but if not:, he asks pardon. How very alien this acknowledgment from the majesty of the Holy Spirit!

In condemning all translations except the Vulgate, as the error is more gross, so the edict is more barbarous. The sacred oracles of God were delivered by Moses and the Prophets in Hebrew, and by the Apostles in Greek. That no corner of the world might be left destitute of so great a treasure, the gift of interpretation was added. It came to pass — I know not by what means, but certainly neither by judgment nor right selection — that of the different versions, one became the favourite of the unlearned, or those at least who, not possessing any knowledge of languages, desired some kind of help to their ignorance. Those, on the other hand, who are acquainted with the languages perceive that this version teems with innumerable errors; and this they make manifest by the clearest evidence. On the other hand, the Fathers of Trent contend, that although the learned thus draw the pure liquor from the very fountain, and convict the infallible Vulgate of falsehood, they are not to be listened to. No man possessed of common sense ever presumed to deprive the Church of God of the benefit of learning. The ancients, though unacquainted with the languages, especially with Hebrew, always candidly acknowledge that nothing is better than to consult the original, in order to obtain the true and genuine meaning. I will go further. There is no man of ordinary talent who, on comparing the

Vulgate version with some others, does not easily see that many things which were improperly rendered by it are in these happily restored. The Council, however, insists that we shall shut our eyes against the light that we may spontaneously go astray.

Who could have imagined they would be so senseless as thus boldly to despise the judgments of good men, and hesitate not to make themselves odious and detestable to all? Those who were aware that they had nothing useful in view, were yet persuaded that they would make some show of it to the world, and assign to some of their sworn adherents the task of executing a new version. In this instance, however, they use no deceit. They not only order us to be contented with a most defective translation, but insist on our worshipping it, just as if it had come down from heaven; and while the blemishes are conspicuous to all, they prohibit us from desiring any improvement. Behold the men on whose judgment the renovation of the Church depends!

It were tedious beyond measure to mark the passages erroneously and absurdly rendered. So far is there from being an entire page, that there are scarcely three continuous verses without some noted blunder. As a specimen, let the Book of Psalms suffice, in which I will touch on a few examples in passing, more to give my readers a sample which may dispose them to ascertain for themselves, than to give full information. In the second Psalm is the well-known exhortation, "Kiss the Son." For this the Vulgate has, "Lay hold of discipline!" There is no resemblance. While the former is clearly correct, why should the latter be held the more authentic? The Vulgate interpreter has,

"Sons of man, how long will you with a heavy heart?" while the Hebrew has nothing like this, but, "How long will ye turn my glory into shame?" (Psalm 4:3.)

Where David complains that his sap was turned into the drought of summer, (Psalm 32:4,) the translator has substituted, "I am turned in my sorrow till the thorn is fixed." Again, in another verse, "In their mouths is bit and bridle to prevent them from approaching thee;" but the translator says, "With hook and rein curb the jaws of those who do not draw near unto thee." And what are we to understand by "lungs filled with illusions," in Psalm 38?

But I act imprudently in entering a boundless forest; I will therefore confine myself to a single Psalm. It will be the sixty-eighth. There David, among the other praises of God, mentions this also, that he makes the single to dwell in a house, i.e., enriches the solitary and childless with a family. The translator substitutes, that he makes them "of one manner." The next words are, "He places the rebellious in a dry parched place." For this the translator has, "In like manner those who exasperate; who dwell in the tombs." Afterward, where the meaning is perfectly obvious in the words of David, the translator makes a riddle fit to puzzle an Oedipus. David says, "The kings of armies have fled, have fled, and the dwellers of the house, i.e., the women who remained at home, have divided the spoil." The translator says, "The king, the virtue of the beloved, beloved, and houses of appearance, have divided the spoil." A little further on, "Though ye have slept among the pots;" translator, "among the clergy!" "To look up to the piled mountains" he substitutes for, "To envy the fertile mountains." Where the Hebrew original has, "Even the rebellious, that God the Lord may dwell," the translator has, "Even those not be-lieving that God the Lord dwells." Again, when the literal meaning is, "I will bring back from Bashan, I will bring back from the depths of the sea," the translator gives the very opposite, "I will turn from Bashan, I will turn into the depth of the sea." Again, "There is little Benjamin their ruler." The translator (I know not what he was thinking of) says, "In excess of mind." I have gone over the half of the Psalm or rather more. What monstrosities do my readers already perceive!

And yet, to confess the truth, there is an excuse for the Latin translator, who gave the meaning of the Greek version as exactly as he could. But who can tolerate those blunderers, who would rob the Church of the gift of interpretation, and thus, as it were, close up the entrance, that none might have access to the pure meaning of David? Add, that they not only prefer the ignorance and blunders of their interpreters to the true renderings of others, but there is no hallucination, however gross, to which they will not give the power of a divine oracle. There is an example of this in Psalm 132. The Lord there promises that he will bless the food of his people. Some luscious priestling, reading the *c* and *t* as one letter, makes the word vidum; but as there is no such word, the insertion of a letter introduced a new reading, which prevails throughout the Papacy, and hence there is no church in Italy, France, Spain, and Germany, in which they do not with loud voice bawl out, "His widow blessing, I will bless." And so attentive and clear-sighted are they, that none of them has observed the ridiculous corruption. But it is not strange that, when they rob us of the word for bread, they introduce the mention of widowhood, since the object on which they are wholly bent is cruelly to bereave souls of the bread of heavenly life. What! are they not ashamed to make the Vulgate version of the New Testament authoritative, while the writings of Valla, Faber, and Erasmus, which are in everybody's hands, demonstrate with the finger, even to children, that it is vitiated in innumerable places? In the first chapter of the Romans the translator calls Christ "the predestinated Son of God." Those not acquainted with Greek are at a loss to explain this term, because, properly speaking, only things which do not yet exist are predestinated; whereas Christ is the eternal Son of God. There is no difficulty in the Greek word, which means "declared."

I have given one example. It were needless labor to give others. In one word, were this edict of the Council sanctioned, the simple effect would be, that the Fathers of Trent would make the world look with their eyes open, and yet not see the light presented to them.

I come to the right of interpreting, which they arrogate to themselves whenever the meaning is doubtful. It is theirs, they say, to give the meaning of Scripture, and we must acquiesce. For everything which they bestow upon the Church they bestow upon themselves. I acknowledge, indeed, that as Scripture, came not by the private will of man, (2 Peter 1:21) it is unbecoming to wrest it to the private sense of any man. Nay, in the case of an obscure passage, when it is doubtful what sense ought to be adopted, there is no better way of arriving at the true meaning than for pious doctors to make common inquiry, by engaging in religious discussion. But that is not now the question. They wish, by their tyrannical edict, to deprive the Church of all liberty, and arrogate to themselves a boundless license; for, be the meaning which they affix to Scripture what it may, it must be immediately embraced. Except themselves, moreover, no man will be permitted to prove anything out of Scripture. Would that they were equal to the performance of so great a task. But oxen usurp the reins, or rather asses the lyre. In short, their aim is to make all revere a Scripture hidden in darkness like the mysteries of Ceres, and let none presume to aspire to the understanding of it.

There would be no end were I to collect all the examples which would make it plain to my readers what fetters of iniquitous and intolerable slavery are forged by this decree. I will therefore give a specimen, in the case of only one Council. About the year 800 was held a Council of Nice, which both restored Images that had been overthrown under Leo and decreed that they were to be worshipped. That Council, because it supports idolatry, the Papists deem holy and lawful. Hence, according to their axiom, it cannot have erred in the exposition of Scripture. But if such interpreters of sacred things are to be listened to, (it is abominable to say they are,) the religion of the Egyptians will be preferable to the Christian. To prove from Scripture that churches were properly adorned with images and pictures, the following passages were adduced:—"God created man after his own image and likeness;" "Joshua erected twelve stones;" "No man lighteth a candle and putteth it under a bushel;" whence they inferred that images were to be placed upon altars! Again, "The light of thy countenance has been stamped upon us:" "as we have heard, so have we also seen;" "O Lord, I have loved the beauty of thy house;" "Show me thy face, for it is lovely." In support of adoration, they wrested the following passages: — "Abraham worshipped the people of the land;" "Jacob set up an inscription, and blessed." Again, "He worshipped the top of the staff of his son Joseph;" "All the rich among the people will deprecate thy countenance;" "Worship his footstool;" "God is to be admired in his saints." And that nothing might be wanting to crown their effrontery, they appended out of another psalm, "His saints who are on the earth." This they applied to images!

I am aware that the narrative I now give will scarcely seem credible. I was myself amazed when I read it, though our ears should long ago have been trained by them to any absurdities, however enormous. Were I to collect all their interpretations, which even children would laugh at, and not even all, but those which are distinguished by some notable absurdity, I would require to form a volume thrice as large as the Bible.

The sum is, that the spirit of Trent wished, by this decree, that Scripture should only signify to us whatever dreaming monks might choose. For what else do they mean by the Church? Though the Roman bishops, I mean all who serve under the banner and auspices of that Anti-Christian See, were to assemble from every quarter of the world, how, pray, could they, by laying their heads together frame a proper version for us? Many of them hardly knew the elements of grammar. At least, they will not venture to deny that there is scarcely one in a hundred who has read an entire book of the Prophets, or one of the Apostolical Epistles, or one of the Gospels. They are too much occupied with other cares to have any leisure for sacred literature. The only resource is, to reserve the privilege for the Apostolic See, and say that the interpretation of Scripture must be sought from the holy lips of Paul Farnese! Otherwise, let them show us a Church which may justly be deemed able to sustain so great a burden. For, how highly soever they may extol the Roman See, they can never persuade some men either that Cephas is its head, or that chaste and holy marriage is the carnal life which is accursed in the sight of God. Both of these have been asserted in Papal responses. They cry out that the whole authority of the Church must fall if it is denied the right of interpreting Scripture — that a door would thus be thrown open to lascivious minds, allowing them to break through every restraint. Nay, in order to cast obloquy upon us, they are wont to charge us with arrogating the interpretation of Scripture to ourselves, in order that there may be no check on our licentiousness. Modesty will not allow me to speak of ourselves as fact would justify; and yet I will most truly declare that we have thrown more light upon the Scriptures than all the doctors who have appeared under the Papacy since its commencement. This praise even they themselves dare not deny us. Still there is none of us who does not willingly submit his lucubrations to the judgment of the Church. Therefore we neither contemn nor impair the authority of the Church; nor do we give loose reins to men to dare what they please. I wish they would show us such a Church as Scripture itself portrays; we should easily agree as to the respect due to it. But when, falsely assuming the name of Church, they seize upon the spoils of which they have robbed it, what else can we do than protest?

FIRST DECREE OF THE FIFTH SESSION OF THE COUNCIL OF TRENT,

HELD JUNE 17, 1546.

That our Catholic Faith, without which it is impossible to please God, may remain in its purity, entire, and untainted, errors being purged away, and that the Christian people may not be carried about by every wind of doctrine, seeing that that old Serpent, the perpetual enemy of the human race, among the very numerous evils with which the Church of God is disturbed in these our days, has stirred up not only new, but also old disputes on the subject of Original Sin, and its remedy; the Holy, Ecumenical, and General Council of Trent, lawfully met in the Holy Spirit, under the presidency of the foresaid Legates of the Apostolic See, desirous to come forward to recall the erring and confirm the wavering, in accordance with the testimony of the Sacred Scriptures, and holy Fathers, and most approved Councils, and the judgment and consent of the Church herself acknowledges, statutes, and declares on the subject of Original Sin, as follows: —

Whosoever confesses not that Adam, the first man, when he had transgressed the command of God in Paradise, instantly lost the holiness and righteousness in which he had been created, and by the guilt of his transgression incurred the wrath and indignation of God, and thereby the death with which God had previously threatened him; and with death captivity under the power of him who thereafter had the empire of death, that is, the devil; and that the whole Adam, by the guilt of that transgression, was changed to the worse in body and soul, let him be anathema.

Whosoever asserts that the transgression of Adam hurt himself only, and not his posterity, and also that he lost for himself alone, and not for us, the holiness and righteousness which he had received from God, or that he, when corrupted, transfused into all the human race by the sin of his disobedience only death and corporal pains, but not sin, which is the death of the soul, let him be anathema, seeing he contradicts the Apostle, who declares, that "by one man sin entered into the world, and death by sin, and so death passed upon all men, inasmuch as all have sinned."

Whosoever asserts that this sin of Adam, which is one by origin, and which transfused, by propagation, not by imitation, is proper to each individual, is taken away either by the power of human nature or by some other remedy than the merit of one Mediator, our Lord Jesus Christ, who reconciled God to us in his own blood, being made unto us righteousness, and sanctification, and redemption; or denies that this merit of Christ Jesus is applied to infants as well as adults by the Sacrament of Baptism duly conferred after the form of the Church, let him be anathema: seeing "there is no other name given under heaven among men, whereby we may be saved." Hence the words, "Behold the Lamb of God; behold him who taketh away the sins of the world;" and "Whosoever of you are baptized, have put on Christ."

Whosoever affirms that new-born infants are not to be baptized, even though they are the children of baptized parents, or says that they are indeed baptized for the remission of sins, but derive no original sin from Adam, which requires to be expiated by the laver of regeneration in order to obtain eternal life — whence it follows, that in them the form of baptism for the remission of sins is not true but false, let him be anathema; seeing that the words of the Apostle, "By one man sin entered into the world, and death by sin, and so death passed upon all men, inasmuch as all have sinned," cannot be understood in any other sense than that in which the Church everywhere diffused has always understood them. By reason of this rule of faith, according to the tradition of the Apostles, even infants who of themselves could not have committed sin, are truly baptized for the remission of sins, in order that what they have contracted by generation may be cleansed by regeneration. For "unless a man be born of water and of the Holy Spirit, he cannot enter the kingdom of God."

Whosoever denies that the guilt of original sin is remitted by the grace of our Lord Jesus Christ, which is conferred in baptism, or even asserts that that which has the true and proper nature of sin is not wholly taken away, but is only rased or not imputed, let him be anathema. For in the regenerate is nothing which God hates, because there is no condemnation in them who have been truly buried with Christ by baptism unto death, who walk not after the flesh; but putting off the old man, and putting on the new man, who is created after God, have been made innocent, unspotted, pure, harmless, and beloved of God, heirs indeed of God and co-heirs with Christ, so that there is nothing to hinder their entrance into heaven. But that concupiscence, or the motions of sin, remain in the baptized, this Holy Council acknowledges and feels; which, as it is left for trial, is not able to hurt those not consenting to it, and manfully withstanding it through the grace of Christ: Nay, he who strives lawfully will be crowned: This concupiscence, which the Apostle sometimes calls sin, the Holy Council declares that the Catholic Church never understood to be called sin, because it is not truly and properly sin in the regenerate, but because it is of sin and inclines to sin. Whoever holds the contrary of this, let him be anathema.

This Holy Council, however, declares that it is not their intention to comprehend in this decree, where it treats of original sin, the blessed and immaculate Virgin Mary, the Mother of God, but that the constitutions of Pope Sixtus IV., of happy memory, are to be observed, under the penalties contained in these constitutions, which the Council renews.

SECOND DECREE OF THE FIFTH SESSION.

T he Holy Council, adhering to the pious constitutions of supreme Pontiffs and approved Councils, and embracing them, and adding to them, in order that the heavenly treasure of the Sacred Books which the Holy Spirit hath, with the greatest liberality delivered to men, may not lie neglected, has statuted and decreed, that in their Churches in which prebends or prestimony, or other stipend, by whatever name called, is found to have been assigned for lecturers on sacred Theology, the Bishops, Archbishops, Primates, and other Ordinaries of the places, shall force and compel those who hold the prebend, prestimony, or stipend, of this description, to expound and interpret the Holy Scripture personally, if they are fit; if otherwise, by a fit substitute to be chosen by the Bishops, Archbishops, Primates, and other Ordinaries of the places, and this under the penalty of sequestering the fruits. In future, let prebends, prestimony, and stipend of this description, be conferred on none but such as are fit and can perform the office in person, and let any appointment made otherwise be null and void.

In Metropolitan or Cathedral Churches, if the city is distinguished or populous, and also in Colleges existing in any important town, though belonging to the diocese, if the clergy there be numerous, where no prebend, prestimony, or stipend of this kind is found to have been assigned, let the first vacant stipend, from whatever cause arising, (resignation excepted,) be understood to be *ipso facto* constituted and assigned in perpetuity to that use. And whenever in the churches themselves there is no prebend, or one that is insufficient, let the Metropolitan, or the Bishop, by the assignation of the fruits of some simple benefice, (subject, however, to the due burdens of the same,) or by the contributions of the beneficiaries of his city or diocese, or otherwise as may be more convenient, provide, with the advice of the Chapter, for the delivery of lectures on the Holy Scriptures, providing always that other lectures, appointed either by custom or in any other way, may not on that account be at all omitted.

Let Churches, when the annual incomes are slender, and the number of clergy and people so small that a lectureship on Theology cannot be conveniently established, at least have a master to be chosen by the Bishop, with the advice of the Chapter, to teach grammar gratis to the clergy and other poor scholars, that, with the will of God, they may pass thereafter to the study of the Holy Scriptures. To that grammar master, therefore, let there be assigned either the fruits of some simple benefice to be drawn by him while he continues to teach, provided always, that the benefice itself be not defrauded of its due service; or let some fit salary be paid from the table of the Chapter or Bishop; or otherwise let the bishop himself adopt some plan suited to his church and diocese, so that this pious, useful, and salutary provision may not on any pretext whatever be neglected.

Also in the Monasteries of Monks, when it can be conveniently, let a Scripture lectureship be established: if in this matter the abbots are neglectful, let the bishops of the diocese see to it that delegates of the Apostolic See may take fit means to compel them.

In the Convents of other Regulars in which literary pursuits may conveniently flourish, let a Scripture lecture be in like manner established, and let this lecture be assigned by the general or provincial chapters to the better qualified masters.

In the Public Schools, where this honorable and of all others most necessary lectureship has not hitherto been appointed, let it be appointed by the piety of most religious princes and states, for the defense and increase of the Catholic faith, and the preservation and propagation of sound doctrine. Where it was appointed, but has fallen into neglect, let it be restored.

And lest impiety be disseminated under the show of piety, the Holy Council enacts that no person shall enter upon this office of lecturing, unless previously tried and approved by the bishop of the place, in respect of life, manners, and knowledge. This, however, is not to be understood of lecturers in the cloisters of monks.

Moreover, let those teaching the Sacred Scriptures, while they teach publicly, in schools, and the scholars who study in these schools, fully possess and enjoy in absence all the privileges conferred by the common law in regard to the drawing of fruits, prebends, and benefices.

But as the preaching; of the Gospel is not less necessary to the Christian commonwealth than lecturing, and is the special office of bishops, the Holy Council has statuted and decreed, that all Bishops, Archbishops,

Primates, and other prelates of churches, shall be bound personally, if under no lawful impediment, to preach the holy Gospel of Jesus Christ.

But if it shall happen that the Bishops and others aforesaid are prevented by a lawful impediment, in accordance with the form of the General Council, they shall be bound to assume fit persons duly to execute this office of preaching. If any one contumaciously refuses to obey, let him be subjected to rigorous punishment.

Let Archpresbyters also, Curates, Parsons parochial, or otherwise holding a cure of souls, by whatever tenure they hold their churches, personally, or if under lawful impediment, by fit persons, at least on the Lord's day, and on solemn feast days, feed the people committed to them, according to their ability, with saving words, by teaching them those things which all must know in order to salvation, and announcing to them with brevity and plainness of speech the vices to be shunned and the virtues to be followed, in order to escape eternal punishment and gain celestial glory. Should any one neglect to perform this duty, though he should claim on some ground or other to be exempted from the jurisdiction of the bishop, or although the churches should be said to be in some way exempted or perhaps annexed and united to some monastery, even situated out of the diocese, still, provided they are locally within the diocese, let the careful pastoral superintendence of the bishops not be wanting, lest the saying should be fulfilled, "The little ones asked for bread, and there was none to break it to them." Wherefore, if after being admonished by the bishop, they continue for three months to fail in their duty, let them be compelled by ecclesiastical censures, or otherwise, at the discretion of the bishop, so that if he shall so deem it expedient some decent salary may be paid out of the fruits of the benefice to another to perform the duty until the principal be brought to repentance and discharge his own office.

Should any Parochial Churches be found subject to monasteries which are not within any diocese, if the abbots and regular prelates shall be negligent in the things aforesaid, let them be compelled by the Metropolitans in whose provinces the dioceses are situated, as *quoad hoc* delegates of the Apostolic See. And let no custom, or exemption, or appeal, or reclamation, or action of recovery, have the effect of staying the execution of this decree, until the matter may have been cognosced and decided by a competent judge, who may proceed summarily on a simple examination of the facts.

But let not the Regulars of any order whatsoever, until they have been examined and approved by their superiors in respect of life, manners, and knowledge, and have obtained a license from them, preach even in the churches of their own orders. With this license they must appear personally before the bishops, and ask their benediction before they begin to preach. But in churches not belonging to their orders, they must, in addition to the license of their superiors, have also the license of the bishop, without which they are on no account to preach in churches not belonging to their orders. The bishops must give this license gratis. Should any Preacher (which God forbid) disseminate errors or scandals among the people, although he preach in a monastery of his own or another order, let the bishop interdict him from preaching; and if he have preached heresy, proceed against him in due course of law, or according to the custom of the place, although the preacher should pretend to be exempted by general or special privilege, in which case let the bishop proceed by apostolic authority as a delegate of the Apostolic See. But let bishops take care that no preacher be slanderously attacked by false information, or otherwise, or have any just ground of complaint.

Let bishops, moreover, beware of allowing any either of those who, though nominally Regulars, live out of the cloister, and without being subject to its rules, or of secular presbyters, unless personally known to them, and of approved learning and character, even under the pretext of any privileges whatsoever, to preach in their city or diocese until the bishops have consulted on the subject with the holy Apostolic See, from which it is not likely that unworthy persons have extorted such privileges unless by concealment of the truth, or direct falsehood.

Eleemosynary Quaestors, commonly called Questuarii, of whatever condition they may be, must not on any account presume to preach, either in person or by the employment of others. Those doing so are by all means to be restrained by proper methods by the bishops and ordinaries of the places, any privileges to the contrary notwithstanding.

This Holy Council statutes and decrees that the next Session shall be held and celebrated on the Thursday after the feast of St. James the Apostle.

ON THE FIRST DECREE OF THE FIFTH SESSION.

That there may be somewhat in this Decree in accordance with the Preface, they borrow the first four heads from the ancient and approved doctrine of the Church. As to these there will be no dispute, and therefore it was obviously malicious in them to premise that their object was to settle the dissensions which have arisen at this time. Of what use was it, pray, to thunder out so many anathemas? Just to make the unskillful believe that there really was some ground for it; though, in fact, there was not. In the fifth head, where they introduce something of their own, they begin to act in their own way, that is, to inculcate the futilities of their sophists, and pertinaciously defend them. They pronounce anathema on any one who denies that everything which has the proper nature of sin is taken away by baptism, and who holds that it is only erased or not imputed. Here they craftily introduce the term erase, which they know to be in bad odor, as the Pelagians annoyed Augustine with it. Let them, therefore, have it their own way, as far as erasing goes.

We assert that the whole guilt of sin is taken away in baptism, so that the remains of sin still existing are not imputed. That this may be more clear, let my readers call to mind that there is a twofold grace in baptism, for therein both remission of sins and regeneration are offered to us. We teach that full remission is made, but that regeneration is only begun and goes on making progress during the whole of life. Accordingly, sin truly remains in us, and is not instantly in one day extinguished by baptism, but as the guilt is effaced it is null in regard to imputation.

Nothing is plainer than this doctrine. Let us see then why it is anathematised by the Council. There is nothing in the regenerate which God hates; so say the venerable Fathers. Were I to grant them this, does it follow that there is nothing deserving of hatred — or is it not rather true that he hates nothing because he pardons what he might justly hate? The passage from the Apostle which they lay hold of plainly supports our view — "There is no condemnation to them who are in Christ Jesus." By these words he does not exempt believers from blame, as if they were pure and free from all sin. He only frees them from guilt, so that while groaning under the burden of sin they are supported by the consolation which he had formerly mentioned, and of which he afterwards discourses more at large, as we shall shortly see. They add, moreover, that there is nothing to stand in the way of their entering heaven. I admit this, not indeed because there is no impediment, but because nothing can hurt those who are clothed with the innocence of Christ. These horned fathers assign a very different reason, viz., because putting off the old man and putting on the new man, who is created after God, they are pure and harmless. Who would not say that they are quibbling? Surely those who are still in the act have not reached the effect. There is therefore a palpable inconsistency in calling those pure and harmless who are still in course of putting off the old man. If they reply, that though they used the present tense they were speaking of the past, I will give them up. For Paul is addressing believers when he bids the Ephesians put off the old man, thereby intimating that the change by which we are renewed from the flesh into the spirit is not the work of one day merely. What have sound readers yet observed in the words quoted by the men of Trent which aids them in the least; nay, where is the quotation that is not utterly opposed to them?

Let us proceed, however, in sifting their decree. They affirm that concupiscence, or the tendency to sin, which they acknowledge to remain in the regenerate, cannot hurt those who do not consent to it, seeing it is left for trial. In other words, it does not hurt, because God perfects his strength in their weakness. But if they insist on its being only a whetstone to sharpen their virtue, Paul erroneously complains that on this very account he was wretched.

But I am foolish in arguing against them from use of the term wretched, while the names of concupiscence, vice, and sin cannot move them. When it is said that pravity in the will is not sin, it might as well be said that man is not an animal; or when it is said that vice is free from blame before God, it might as well be said that the sun is not a shining body. What shall I say of the term sin? They quibble and say that Paul here used the term for the cause and punishment of sin: as if this were not clearly at variance with the context. After mentioning sin he immediately adds, "I find a law, that when I would do good evil is present with me." Do they think that this is also spoken improperly? If it were only a verbal question, still they ought no more to be listened to than those who affirm that infants cannot properly be said to be born with sin. Both interpret sin in the same way. There is this difference, that the latter speak thus of original sin generally, whereas these venerable Fathers maintain that after baptism a thing is no longer the same thing it was, though it remains the same. If they would better their case, they must first of all show that there is such a conversion in the nature of things that what is the same becomes unlike itself. But the slightest consideration of the matter removes all dispute. It cannot be denied without effrontery, that repugnance to the law of God is truly sin. But the Apostle affirms this of a disease remaining in the regenerate. It follows, therefore, that of its own nature it is sin, although it is not imputed, and the guilt is abolished by the grace of Christ. If the true standard of righteousness is to love God with the whole heart, and mind, and strength, it is clear that the heart cannot incline otherwise without declining from righteousness. Paul complains that he is hindered from doing the good which he would do. The law, I say, requires perfect love: we do not yield it. Our duty was to run, and we go on slowly limping. In this defect the venerable fathers find nothing which ought to be considered sin.

With the same dishonesty they declare that the Church never understood otherwise. But Ambrose, as Augustine testifies, distinctly calls it "unrighteousness." What says Augustine himself? There are many passages in which his acknowledgment of this appears without obscurity. As when he says, in the second book against Julian, that "in baptism the law of sin is remitted, not ended." Again, "The guilt is loosed, the thing remains." Again, "Sin is dead in the guilt by which it held us, but the dead rebels until cured by the finished work of sepulture." Again, in the homily on John, on the first of Lent, "As long as you live sin must be in your members. At Lent let it be deprived of dominion: do not as it bids." But of many passages it will be sufficient to adduce one which seems to have been written for the express purpose of refuting their folly. In the fifth book against Julian he names three reasons why it is called sin, even in the regenerate. The words are, "As blindness of heart is the sin by which we believe not in God, and the punishment of sin by which the proud heart receives condign chastisement, and the cause of sin when through the error of a blind heart any offense is committed, so the concupiscence of the flesh, which the Good Spirit resists, is also sin, because there is disobedience in it against the dominion of the mind, and the punishment of sin because inflicted on the demerits of the disobedient, and the cause of sin from defect of will or corruption of nature." A meaning, which the Council declares to have been unknown to the early Church, every one here sees set down as the primary meaning by the most competent witness of antiquity. The definition of the Council will be mighty indeed if it can make darkness out of this clear light, and so fascinate the eyes of men as to make them think they are looking at one thing when they see another.

ON THE SECOND DECREE OF THE FIFTH SESSION.

I should like first to know what approved Councils there are which they join with Sovereign Pontiffs? For at the time when lawful Councils of good fame were held no man was acknowledged as sovereign pontiff, nor even as first bishop; for this was expressly forbidden in the Council of Carthage. Accordingly we see that the Councils to which this specious coloring is given, are no other than six or seven spurious Councils held after the light of sound doctrine was extinguished, and discipline had decayed, and when the merest dolts were present — Councils which exhibit no appearance of ancient dignity, but smack of the Gothic tyranny of the Roman See. Fine Reformers, truly! See how things which the Lateran Council raked together from the foul dregs of a most corrupt age, and which posterior Councils made even worse, are here brought forward to claim new honors! But I mistake, for they distinctly avow that they will make I know not what additions to them. To know the quality of these additions we must look at the decrees.

They enjoin, that those who hold prebends intended for lecturers on sacred theology shall perform the office of teaching either themselves or by others if they are unfit. The Council thus leaves men who are unlearned and utterly unfit in possession of the place which they have usurped by fraud, injustice, and sacrilege, without any appearance of law, provided they bestow some small portion of the stipend on substitutes. But they carefully provide that in future none but fit persons shall be admitted! By whose judgment? To whom could they assign the task but to the canonical authorities of the districts? A bishop therefore is to elect any kind of reader he pleases. What Chapter will be so harsh as not to be satisfied with any person, whatever his qualifications? But if he happens to be disapproved, litigation will arise. Unless something miraculous occur the nomination of the bishop will be sustained. Then what is to be the course of lectures? what the time? what the auditory? As to all these things the venerable fathers are prudently silent, in order to persuade the simple they were doing something when they were doing nothing. What! is not the thing which they prescribe already common? The lecturer, in order merely to preserve the emolument, every week invites two or three of his boon companions, and makes a mere show of lecturing.

In the second chapter they appoint new lectures. Where? In Metropolitan or Episcopal Churches, but only if the city be of note and populous. No doubt they were afraid lest the audience should freeze if the places were less distinguished. This, however, is just as much as saying nothing; but they wish the same rule to be observed in distinguished towns. They say this, but what plan do they propose? That either the bishop assign a stipend out of a simple benefice, or the clergy of the diocese contribute, or some other plan be adopted by the canons. These alternatives can have no other effect than to put the thing off for ages.

To the same effect is their enactment about teachers; for there is no ground to hope that the incomes of priests will be employed in that way; far less that the bishops will curtail their table in the least. The third plan remaining is for the bishop to devise some method. But before the litigation between him and the clergy on the subject of contribution is ended, the memory of the Council of Trent will be buried in oblivion. The worthy decretists are not ignorant of this; but it was necessary to adopt some fiction, so as not to leave it perfectly apparent that nothing was done.

If the fourth chapter be read cursorily, it might cause no little alarm to the monks, lest they should be sent back to theological studies. But there are two exceptions which rid them of their fear. First, they ordain lectures only when it will be convenient. But there is no monastery which is not as inhospitable to all kinds of liberal study as if it were a den of Cyclops. The second exception makes them still safer. Command is given to the bishops to use compulsion with the abbots if they are negligent. And they are to do this as if they were delegates of the Apostolic See. Therefore, whenever any bishop proves troublesome to an abbot, an appeal will be taken, and the cause will be pleaded at Rome. What will the issue be? The monks will sooner swallow the whole volume of Scripture than be forced to hear one lecture!

Moreover, that no celebrated School may be without a theological lecture, they exhort sovereigns and states to contribute the expense; as if this perfunctory recommendation were to have much weight, especially when it is clear enough that an hundred times more is swallowed up by lazybellies than would serve the purpose. Why, then, do they not command it to be taken from that quarter, but just because their real intention is that nothing shall be done

As the rest are of the same description, there is no use in wasting good time in the discussion of such trifling. It is quite certain that they wished by a profusion of words to blind the eyes of the simple, and make them believe that they were something to the purpose, until experience should teach them how they had been deluded. Every one who has an ounce of sound judgment will acknowledge with me, that the whole is nothing better than a mere sound of words, which they who use them have no wish to be heard.

SIXTH SESSION OF THE COUNCIL OF TRENT.

A s at this time, not without the loss of souls and grievous detriment to ecclesiastical unity, certain erroneous views have been disseminated concerning The Doctrine of Justification, the Holy, Ecumenical, and General Council of Trent, lawfully met in the Holy Spirit, with the most reverend Lords, John Maria del Monte, bishop of Praeneste, and Marcellus, with the tide of the Holy Cross in Jerusalem, Presbyters, Cardinals of the, Roman Church, and Apostolic Legates *de latere*, presiding in the name of the most Holy Father in Christ, our Lord Paul III., Pope, by Divine Providence, purposes, with a view to the praise and glory of Almighty God, the tranquility of the Church, and the salvation of souls, to expound to all the faithful of Christ the true and sound Doctrine of Justification, which Christ the Sun of righteousness, the author and finisher of our faith taught, the Apostles delivered, and the Catholic

Church, under the guidance of the Holy Spirit, hath constantly retained; strictly prohibiting any one from daring henceforth to believe, preach, or teach, otherwise than is statuted and declared by the present Decree.

OF THE INCAPABILITY OF NATURE AND THE LAW TO JUSTIFY MEN.

II. The Holy Council declares that to understand the doctrine of Justification properly and purely, it is necessary for every one to acknowledge and confess, that when all had lost their innocence by the transgression of Adam, had become impure, and as the Apostle says, by nature children of wrath, as has been explained in the decree concerning Original Sin, they were so much the servants of sin and under the power of the devil and of death, that not only the Gentiles by the power of nature, but even the Jews by the very letter of the law of Moses, could not be freed therefrom, or rise, notwithstanding that free-will was by no means extinguished in them, though weakened in its powers and under a bias.

OF THE DISPENSATION AND MINISTRY OF THE ADVENT OF CHRIST.

III. To which it was owing:, that our Heavenly Father, the Father of mercies, and God of all consolation, when that blessed fullness of the times was come, sent to men Christ Jesus his Son, both before the Law and in the time of the Law, declared and promised to many holy fathers, to redeem the Jews who were under the Law, and that the Gentiles who did not follow righteousness, might obtain righteousness, and all receive the adoption of sons. Him God set forth to be a propitiation through faith in his blood for our sins, and not only for ours, but also for the sins of the whole world.

WHO ARE JUSTIFIED BY CHRIST.

IV. But though He died for all, all do not receive the benefit of his death, but those only to whom the merit of his passion is communicated. For as in truth men, if they were not born by propagation from the seed of Adam, would not be born unrighteous, while by that propagation, from the mere fact of their conception, they contract a proper unrighteousness; so, unless they were born again in Christ, they would never be justified, seeing that new birth is given them through the merit of his passion, by the grace by which they are made righteous. For this benefit the Apostle exhorts us always to give thanks to the Father who hath made us meet to partake of the inheritance of the saints in light, and hath rescued us from the power of darkness, and transferred us into the kingdom of the Son of his love, in whom we have redemption and the forgiveness of sins.

IMPLIED DESCRIPTION OF THE JUSTIFICATION OF THE UNGODLY, AND THE METHOD OF IT IN A STATE OF GRACE.

V. In these words there is an implied description of the Justification of the ungodly, viz., that it is a translation from that state in which man, the son of the first Adam, is born to a state of grace, and the adoption of sons by the second Adam, Jesus Christ our Savior; which translation, since the Gospel was promulgated, cannot be effected without the law of regeneration, or the wish for it; as it is written, "Unless a man be born again," etc.

OF THE NECESSITY OF PREPARATION IN ADULTS FOR JUSTIFICATION, AND WHENCE IT IS.

VI. The Council declares that the commencement of this Justification in adults is to be derived from the preventing grace of God through Jesus Christ; that is, from his calling, by which they are called without any existing merits of their own, so that those who, by sins, were alienated from God, are, by his exciting and assisting grace, disposed to turn in order to their own justification, by assenting freely to the same grace, and cooperating with it. Thus, while God touches the heart of man by the illumination of his Spirit, man himself does nothing at all in receiving that inspiration, for he can reject it; and yet he cannot of his own free will, without the grace of God, make a movement towards justification before him. Hence, in the Sacred Scriptures, when it is said, "Turn ye unto me, and I will turn unto you," we are reminded of our freedom; and when we reply, "Turn thou us, O Lord, and we shall be turned," we acknowledge that we are prevented by the grace of God.

THE MODE OF JUSTIFICATION.

VII. Men are disposed to righteousness when awakened and aided by divine grace, and conceiving faith from hearing, they are freely moved towards God, believing those things to be true which have been divinely revealed and promised, and specially this, that the wicked is justified of God by his grace through the redemption which is in Christ Jesus; and while perceiving that they are sinners, turning from the fear of the divine justice, by which they are beneficially alarmed to consider the mercy of God, they are raised to hope, trusting that God will be propitious to them through Christ, and they begin to love him as the source of all righteousness; and they are thus moved against sin by some hatred and detestation, that is, by that penitence which ought to be performed before baptism; in short, while they purpose to receive baptism, to begin a new life, and observe the divine commandments. Of this disposition it is written, "He that cometh to God must believe that he is, and that he is the rewarder of those who seek him;" and, "Be of good courage, son, thy sins are forgiven thee;" and, "The fear of the Lord expels sin;" "Repent and be baptized, every one of you, in the name of Jesus Christ, and ye shall receive the forgiveness of your sins, and the gift of the Holy

Spirit;" "Go and teach all nations, baptizing them in the name of the Father, and the Son, and the Holy Ghost, teaching them to observe all things whatsoever I have commanded you;" finally, "Prepare your hearts for the Lord," etc..

WHAT IS THE JUSTIFICATION OF THE UNGODLY MAN, AND WHAT ARE ITS CAUSES.

VIII. This preparation or disposition is followed by Justification, which is not the mere forgiveness of sins, but also Sanctification, and the renewal of the inner man, by the voluntary reception of grace and gifts; whence the man from unrighteous becomes righteous, from an enemy becomes a friend, so as to be heir according to the hope of eternal life. The causes of Justification are these: — The final cause is the glory of God and Christ, and eternal life: the efficient cause is a merciful God, who freely washes and sanctifies, sealing and anointing with the Holy Spirit of promise, which is a pledge of our inheritance: The meritorious cause is his beloved, only-begotten Son, our Lord Jesus Christ, who, when we were enemies, because of the great love wherewith he loved us, by his own most holy passion on the wood of the cross, merited justification, and gave satisfaction to the Father for us: The instrumental cause is the sacrament of baptism, which is the sacrament of faith, without which justification is never obtained: In fine, the only formal cause is the righteousness of God, not that by which he himself is righteous, but that by which he makes us righteous, i.e., by which he presents us with it, we are renewed in the spirit of our mind, and are not only reputed, but are truly called and are righteous, each one of us receiving his righteousness in ourselves according to the measure which the Holy Spirit imparts to each as he pleases, and according to the proper disposition and co-operation of each. For although no man can be righteous unless the merits of Christ's passion are communicated to him, that takes place in this

Justification of the ungodly, when, by the merit of the same holy passion, the love of God is diffused by the Holy Spirit in the hearts of those who are justified, and inheres in them. Hence, in Justification itself, along with the remission of sins, man receives, through Jesus Christ, in whom he is ingrafted, all these things infused at the same time, viz., faith, hope, and charity; for faith, unless hope and charity are added to it, neither unites perfectly with Christ, nor forms a living member of his body; for which reason it is most truly said that faith without works would be dead and inoperative, and that in Christ Jesus neither circumcision nor uncircumcision availeth anything, but faith which worketh by love. This faith, before the sacrament of baptism, catechumens, in accordance with the tradition of the Apostles, seek from the Church when they seek faith producing eternal life; which life faith cannot produce without hope and charity. Hence also they immediately hear the words of Christ, "If ye would enter into life, keep the commandments." Therefore, receiving true and Christian righteousness as a first robe, instead of that one which Adam lost by his disobedience — lost both for himself and for us — a fair and immaculate robe, presented to them by Jesus Christ, which, on being born again, they are enjoined to preserve, that they may produce it before the tribunal of our Lord Jesus Christ, and have eternal life.

IN WHAT WAY IT IS TO BE UNDERSTOOD THAT THE UNGODLY MAN IS JUSTIFIED BY FAITH, AND FREELY.

IX. When the Apostle says that a man is Justified by Faith, and Freely, the words, are to be understood in that sense which the perpetual sense of the Catholic Church has held and expressed, viz., that we are, therefore, said to be justified by faith, because faith is the beginning of salvation, the foundation and root of all justification, without which it is impossible to please God and attain to the fellowship of the Son of God. And we are said to be justified freely, because none of those things which precede justification, whether faith or works, merit the grace of justification itself; for if it be of grace, it is no longer of works, otherwise grace were no more grace.

AGAINST THE VAIN CONFIDENCE OF HERETICS.

X. But although it is necessary to believe that sins neither are remitted, nor have ever been remitted, except freely by the Divine mercy through Christ, it is not to be said to any one boasting a confidence and certainty of the forgiveness of his sins, that his sins are forgiven, or have been forgiven; seeing this vain confidence, totally remote from piety, may exist in heretics and schismatics, nay, in our own time does exist, and is extolled with great hostility to the Catholic Church. Neither is it to be asserted that it becomes those who are truly justified to determine with themselves, without any kind of doubt, that they are truly justified, and that no man is absolved from sin and justified, save he who assuredly believes that he is acquitted and justified, and that acquittal and justification are obtained by this faith alone; as if any one who does not believe this were doubting the promise of God and the efficacy of the death and resurrection of Christ. For as no pious man ought to doubt of the mercy of God, the merit of Christ, and the virtue and efficacy of the sacraments, so every one, while he beholds his own weakness and disinclination, may be in fear and dread respecting his own gracious state; seeing that no man can know with a certainty of faith, as to which there can be no lurking error, that he has obtained the grace of God.

OF THE INCREASE OF RECEIVED JUSTIFICATION.

XI. Having been thus justified and become the friends and of the household of God, going on from strength to strength, they are, as the Apostle says, renewed from day to day, that is, mortifying the members of their flesh, and displaying those weapons of righteousness received from God for sanctification, by the observance of the commandments of

God and of the Church in righteousness itself, through the grace of Jesus Christ. Faith cooperating with good works, they grow and are justified more and more, as it is written, "Let him who is just be justified still;" and again, "Fear not to be justified even unto death;" and again, "You see how a man is justified by works and not by faith only." This increase of righteousness the holy Church begs, when she prays, "Lord increase our faith, hope, and charity," etc.

OF THE OBSERVANCE OF THE COMMANDMENTS — ITS NECESSITY AND POSSIBILITY.

XII. No man, however justified, should think himself free from the observance of the Commandments; no man should use that presumptuous expression prohibited under anathema by the Fathers, that to a justified man the precepts of God are impossible of observance; for God does not order what is impossible, but by ordering admonishes you both to do what you can, and ask what you cannot, and assists, that you may be able to do. His commandments are not grievous; his yoke is easy, and his burden is light. For those who are of God love Christ, and those who love him, as he himself testifies, keep his commandments, as indeed they can do, with the Divine assistance. For in this mortal life, however just and holy they may be, they may fall into light and daily sins, which are also called venial; and when they do fall they do not thereby cease to be righteous, for those words are used by the righteous, and are both humble and true, "Forgive us our debts." Hence it follows that the righteous ought to feel themselves under a greater obligation to walk in the way of righteousness, in that being freed from sin and become the servants of God, living soberly, righteously, and godly, they may be able to make progress through Jesus Christ, by whom they have access into that grace: for God does not forsake those once justified by his grace, unless he is previously forsaken by them.

Wherefore no man ought to flatter himself in Faith alone, thinking that by faith alone he has been appointed heir, and will obtain the inheritance, although he do not suffer with Christ, that he may also be glorified with him. For Christ himself, though he was the Son of God, learned obedience from the things Which he suffered; and being made consummate, became the author of eternal life to all who obey him. Accordingly the Apostle himself admonishes the justified, saying, "Know you not that of those who run in a race all indeed run, but one receives the prize? So run that you may obtain. I therefore so run not as uncertainly, so fight, not as beating the air; but I chastise my body and reduce it into subjection, lest when I have preached to others I should myself be made a reprobate." Again, Peter, the prince of the Apostles, says, "Endeavor by good works to make your calling and election sure, for so doing, you will never sin." Whence it is evident that those oppose the orthodox doctrine of religion who say that in every good work the religious man sins at least venially, or, what is more intolerable, deserves eternal punishment; as also those who hold that in all works the righteous sin, if, while stirring up their sluggishness, and exhorting themselves to run the race, they, though doing so primarily in order that God may be glorified, have also an eye to the eternal reward; seeing it is written, "I have inclined my heart to do thy righteousness, because of recompense;" and the Apostle says of Moses, that "he looked to the reward."

AS TO PREDESTINATION, IT IS NECESSARY TO GUARD AGAINST RASH PRESUMPTION.

XIII. No man also, so long as he lives in this mortal life, should presume so far on the secret mystery of Predestination as to determine for certain that he himself is in the number of the predestinated; as if it were true that a justified man can no more sin, or, if he sin, may promise himself certain repentance. For it cannot be known without special revelation who they are whom God has chosen to himself.

OF THE GIFT OF PERSEVERANCE.

XIV. The same is true in regard to the gift of Perseverance, of which it is written, "He who perseveres unto the end shall be saved:" a thing indeed which cannot be obtained anywhere else than from Him who is powerful to make him who stands stand perseveringly, and restore him who falls. Let no man promise himself anything with absolute certainty, although all ought to place and repose the firmest hope in the help of God. For God, if they themselves are not wanting to his grace, will, as he has begun the good work, also finish it, working in them to will and to do. Still let those who think they stand take heed lest they fall, and with fear and trembling work out their salvation, in labors, in vigils, and alms, in prayers and oblations, in fastings and chastity. For knowing that they have been born again to the hope of glory, but not yet to glory, they ought to be in fear concerning the contest which remains with the devil, the world, and the flesh; in which they cannot be victorious, unless, by the grace of God, they obey the Apostle when he says, "We are debtors not to the flesh to live after the flesh; for if ye live after the flesh ye shall die, but if by the Spirit ye mortify the deeds of the flesh, ye shall live."

OF THE LAPSED AND THEIR RECOVERY.

XV. Those who, after receiving the grace of Justification, have fallen through sin, may again be justified, when God arousing them by the sacrament of penitence, they shall have succeeded, by the merit of Christ, in recovering lost grace. For this restoration of the fallen is a mode of justification, and has been aptly called by the Fathers a second plank after shipwreck of lost grace. For in behalf of those who fall into sin after baptism, Christ Jesus instituted the sacrament of penitence, where he says, "Receive the Holy Spirit: whose sins ye remit they are remitted to them, and whose sins ye retain they are retained." Whence it follows, that the penitence of a Christian man after a lapse is very different from the baptismal; and consists not only in a cessation from sin and detestation of it, or in a humbled and contrite heart, but also in a sacramental confession of sin, to be made at least in wish, and in its own time, and in sacerdotal absolution; likewise in satisfaction by fasting, alms, prayer, and other pious exercises of the spiritual life: not indeed for the eternal punishment, which even by a wish for the sacrament is remitted along with the guilt, but the temporal punishment, which, as the Scriptures say, is not always, as in baptism, entirely remitted to those who, ungrateful for the grace of God which they received, have grieved the Holy Spirit, and not feared to pollute the temple of God. Of this penitence it is written, "Remember, whenever ye have fallen, repent and do the first works." Again, "The sorrow which is according to God worketh repentance for a stable salvation." And again, "Repent, and bring forth fruits worthy of repentance."

THAT BY ANY MORTAL SIN GRACE IS LOST, BUT NOT FAITH.

XVI. In opposition to the craftiness of certain men who, by smooth speeches and fair words, seduce the hearts of the simple, it is to be asserted, that not only by unbelief, by which even faith itself is lost, but also by any other mortal sin, though faith is not lost, the Grace received in justification is lost: thus defending the doctrine of the Divine law, which excludes from the kingdom of heaven, not only unbelievers, but also believers who are fornicators, adulterers, effeminate, abusers of themselves with mankind, thieves, misers, drunkards, evil speakers, plunderers, and all others who commit deadly sins, from which, by the help of Divine grace, they are able to abstain, and the effect of which is to separate them from the grace of Christ.

OF THE FRUIT OF JUSTIFICATION, THAT IS, OF THE MERIT OF GOOD WORKS, AND OF THE NATURE OF MER-IT ITSELF.

XVII. To men justified in this way, whether they have constantly preserved the grace received, or recovered it when lost, are to be set forth these words of the Apostle, "Abound in every good work, knowing that your labor is not in vain in the Lord; for God is not unjust to forget your work and love which ye have shown in his name:" and "Lose not your confidence, which has great recompense." To those, therefore, who work well even unto the end and hope in God, is to be held forth eternal life both as a gift mercifully promised to the children of God through Jesus Christ, and as a reward faithfully to be paid according to the promise of God to their good works and merits. For this is the crown of righteousness, which, after their contest and race, is, as the Apostle says, set apart for them, to be bestowed on them by the just Judge, and not only on them, but on all who love his advent. For seeing that Christ himself, as the head to the members and the vine to the branches, is perpetually infusing his virtue into the justified — a virtue which always precedes, accompanies, and follows their good works, and without these works cannot in any way be agreeable to God and meritorious, it must be believed that nothing more is wanting to the justified to enable them by those works which are done in God, fully to satisfy the Divine law according to the state of this life, and truly to merit the obtaining of eternal life in due time, provided they die in grace: since Christ our Savior says, "If any one drink of the water which I will give him, he shall never thirst, but it will become in him a fountain of water springing up unto everlasting life." Thus neither is our own righteousness established as if it were properly of us, nor is the righteousness of God overlooked or repudiated: for the righteousness which is called ours, inasmuch as by it inhering in us we are justified, is also the righteousness of God, because infused into us by God through the merits of Christ.

This, however, must not be omitted. Although so much is attributed to good works in Scripture, that Christ promises that he who has given a cup of cold water to one of his disciples shall not go unrewarded, and the Apostle testifies that our light momentary tribulation at present is working in us an exceedingly sublime, an eternal weight of glory; far be it from any Christian man to confide or glory in himself, and not in the Lord, whose goodness towards all men is so great that he is pleased to regard his own gifts as their merits. And as we all offend in many things, every one of us ought to have before his eyes, besides mercy and goodness, judgment and severity; nor ought any one, though he may not be conscious of anything, to judge himself, since the whole lives of men must be tried and judged not by human judgment, but by the judgment of God, who will bring to light the hidden things of darkness, and manifest the counsels of the heart: and then shall every one have praise of God, who, as it is written, will render to every man according to his works.

After this Catholic doctrine of Justification, which, unless a man believe faithfully and firmly, he cannot be justified, it has pleased the Holy Council to subjoin the following Canons, that all may know not only what they ought to hold and follow, but also what to shun and avoid.

CANONS.

I. Whosoever shall say that a man can be justified by his works, which are done either by the powers of human nature or the teaching of the law without divine grace through Christ, let him be anathema.

II. Whosoever shall say that Divine grace by Jesus Christ is given for this purpose only, that men may be able to live righteously and merit eternal life, as if he could do both by free-will without grace, though scarcely and with difficulty, let him be anathema.

III. Whosoever shall say that without the preventing inspiration of the Holy Spirit and His assistance, man can believe, hope, love, or repent, so that the grace of justification behooves to be conferred upon him, let him be anathema.

IV. Whosoever shall say that the free-will of man, moved and excited by God, does not at all co-operate with God when exciting and calling, that thus he may dispose and prepare himself for obtaining the grace of justification, and that he cannot dissent though he wills it, but like something inanimate does nothing at all, and acts passively merely, let him be anathema.

V. Whosoever shall say that the free-will of man was lost and extinguished after Adam's sin, or that it is a thing of name merely, or a name without a thing, in short, a figment introduced into the Church by Satan, let him be anathema.

VI. Whosoever shall say that it is not in the power of man to make his ways evil, but that God produces bad works as well as good, not permissively only, but properly and of himself, so that the treachery of Judas is no less his proper work than the calling of Paul, let him be anathema.

VII. Whosoever shall say that all the works which are done before justification, on whatever account they may be done, are truly sins, and deserve the hatred of God, or that the more vehemently a man tries to dispose himself for grace, the more grievously he sins, let him be anathema.

VIII. Whosoever shall say that the fear of hell, by which we flee to the mercy of God, grieving for our sins, or by which we abstain from sinning, is sin, or makes sinners worse, let him be anathema.

IX. Whosoever shall say that the wicked is justified by faith alone, in such a sense that nothing else is required in the way of co-operation to obtain the grace of justification, and that it is in no respect necessary that he be prepared and disposed by the movement of his own will, let him be anathema.

X. Whosoever shall say that men are justified without the righteousness of Christ, by which He merited for us, or that by that righteousness they are formally righteous, let him be anathema.

XI. Whosoever shall say that men are justified by the mere imputation of Christ's righteousness, or by the mere remission of sins, exclusive of grace and charity which is shed abroad in their hearts by the Holy Spirit, and is inherent in them, or also, that the grace by which we are justified is only the favor of God, let him be anathema

XII. Whosoever shall say that justifying faith is nothing else than trust in the Divine mercy forgiving sins by Christ, or that this trust is the only thing by which we are justified, let him be anathema.

XIII. Whosoever shall say that for any man to obtain the remission of sins, it is necessary to believe for a certainty and without any hesitancy, as to his own weakness and disinclination that his sins are forgiven, let him be anathema.

XIV. Whosoever shall say that a man is absolved from his sins, or justified by the mere circumstance of believing for a certainty that he is absolved or justified, or that no man is truly justified save he who believes that he is justified, and that acquittal and absolution are accomplished by faith alone, let him be anathema.

XV. Whosoever shall say that a man regenerated or justified, is bound in faith to believe that he is certainly in the number of the predestinated, let him be anathema.

XVI. Whosoever shall say that he holds it absolutely and infallibly certain that he shall have the great gift of perseverance even unto the end, if he has not learned this by special revelation, let him be anathema.

XVII. Whosoever shall say that the grace of justification falls to none but those predestinated unto life, and that all others who are called are called indeed, but do not receive grace, as being predestinated by the Divine power to evil, let him be anathema.

XVIII. Whosoever shall say that the commandments of God are impossible of observance even to a justified man, and to one constituted under grace, let him be anathema

XIX. Whosoever shall say that nothing is commanded in the gospel except faith; that other things are indifferent, being neither commanded nor prohibited, but free; or that the ten commandments do not apply to Christians, let him be anathema.

XX. Whosoever shall say that a justified man, however perfect, is not bound to the observance of the commandments of God and the Church, but only to believe as if the gospel were a naked and absolute promise of eternal life, without the condition of observing the commandments, let him be anathema.

XXI. Whosoever shall say that Jesus Christ was given by God to man as a Redeemer in whom they may trust, but not as a lawgiver whom they are to obey, let him be anathema.

XXII. Whosoever shall say that a justified man, even without the special assistance of God, is able to persevere in received righteousness, or with the assistance of God is not able, let him be anathema.

XXIII. Whosoever shall say that a man once justified cannot sin any more or lose grace, and therefore that he who falls or sins was never truly justified, or that he is able during his whole life to avoid all sins, even venial, unless it be by the special privilege of God, as the Church holds concerning the blessed Virgin, let him be anathema.

XXIV. Whosoever shall say that received righteousness is not preserved and even is not increased in the view of God by good works, that works themselves are only the fruits and signs of justification obtained, but not the cause of increasing it, let him be anathema.

XXV. Whosoever shall say that in every work whatever the just man sins, at least venially, or, which is more intolerable, mortally, and thereby deserves eternal punishment. let him be anathema.

XXVI. Whosoever shall say that the righteous ought not, for the good works which may have been done in God, to expect and hope for eternal recompense from God through his mercy and the merits of Jesus Christ, if he persevere even to the end in well-doing and in keeping the Divine commandments, let him be anathema.

XXVII. Whosoever shall say that there is no mortal sin but that of unbelief, and that by no sin, however grievous and enormous, save that of infidelity, can grace once received be lost, let him be anathema.

XXVIII. Whosoever shall say that grace being lost by sin, faith is lost at the same time and for ever, or that the faith which remains is not true faith, though it be not lively, or that he who has faith without charity is not a Christian, let him be anathema.

XXIX. Whosoever shall say that he who has fallen after baptism cannot rise again by the grace of God, or that he may indeed, but by faith alone, recover lost righteousness without the sacrament of penitence, as the Holy Roman and Universal Church taught by Christ the Lord and his Apostles hath hitherto professed, observed, and taught, let him be anathema.

XXX. Whosoever shall say that after the grace of justification has been received, the guilt or liability to eternal punishment is so remitted to every penitent sinner, that no liability to temporal punishment remains to be discharged either in this world or in the next in purgatory, before he can obtain access to the kingdom of heaven, let him be anathema.

XXXI. Whosoever shall say that a justified man sins when, he does good works with a view to eternal reward, let him be anathema.

XXXII. Whosoever shall say that the good works of a justified man are in such a sense the gifts of God, that they are not good merits of the justified man himself, or that a justified man by good works which are done by him through the grace of God and the merits of Jesus Christ, of which he is a living member, does not truly merit increase of grace, eternal life, and the actual attainment of eternal life if he die in grace, together with increase of glory, let him be anathema.

XXXIII. Whosoever shall say that this Catholic doctrine of justification expressed by the Holy Council in this present decree, derogates in any respect from the glory of God or the merits of our Lord Jesus Christ, and does not rather illustrate the truth of our faith, in short, the glory of God and of Jesus. Christ, let him be anathema

ON THE SIXTH SESSION OF THE COUNCIL OF TRENT.

T he doctrine of man's Justification would be easily explained, did not the false opinions by which the minds of men are preoccupied, spread darkness over the clear light. The principal cause of obscurity, however, is, that we are with the greatest difficulty induced to leave the glory of righteousness entire to God alone. For we always desire to be somewhat, and such is our folly, we even think we are. As this pride was innate in man from the first, so it opened a door for Satan to imbue them with many impious and vicious conceits with which we have this day to contend. And in all ages there have been sophists exercising their pen in extolling human righteousness, as they knew it would be popular. When by the singular kindness of God, the impiety of Pelagius was repudiated with the common consent of the ancient Church, they no longer dared to talk so pertly of human merit. They, however, devised a middle way, by which they might not give God the whole in justification, and yet give something. This is the moderation which the venerable Fathers adopt to correct the errors on Justification, which, they say, have arisen in our day. Such indeed is their mode of prefacing, that at the outset they breathe nothing but Christ; but when they come to the subject, far are they from leaving him what is his own. Nay, their definition at length contains nothing else than the trite dogma of the schools: that men are justified partly by the grace of God and partly by their own works; thus only showing themselves somewhat more modest than Pelagius was.

This will easily be shown to be the fact. For under the second head, where they treat of Original Sin, they declare that free-will, though impaired in its powers and biassed, is not however extinguished. I will not dispute about a name, but since they contend that liberty has by no means been extinguished, they certainly understand that the human will has still some power left to choose good. For where death is not, there is at least some portion of life. They themselves remove all ambiguity when they call it impaired and biassed. Therefore, if we believe them, Original Sin has weakened us, so that the defect of our will is not pravity but weakness. For if the will were wholly depraved, its health would not only be impaired but lost until it were renewed. The latter, however, is uniformly the doctrine of Scripture. To omit innumerable passages where Paul discourses on the nature of the human race, he does not charge free-will with weakness, but declares all men to be useless, alienated from God, and enslaved to the tyranny of sin; so much so, that he says they are unfit to think a good thought. (Romans 3:12; 2 Corinthians 3:5.) We do not however deny, that a will, though bad, remains in man. For the fall of Adam did not take away the will, but made it a slave where it was free. It is not only prone to sin, but is made subject to sin. Of this subject we shall again speak by and bye.

The third and fourth heads I do not touch. Towards the end of the fifth head they affirm that no transference to a state of grace takes place without Baptism, or a wish for it. Would it not have been better to say, that by the word and sacraments Christ is communicated, or, if they prefer so to speak, applied to us, than to make mention of baptism alone? But they have been pleased to exclude infants from the kingdom of God, who have been snatched away before they could be offered for baptism. As if nothing were meant when it is said that the children of believers are born holy. (1 Corinthians 7:14.) Nay, on what ground do we admit them to baptism unless that they are the heirs of promise? For did not the promise of life apply to them it would be a profanation of baptism to give it to them. But if God has adopted them into his kingdom, how great injustice is done to his promise, as if it were not of itself sufficient for their salvation! A contrary opinion, I admit, has prevailed, but it is unjust to bury the truth of God under any human error, however ancient. The salvation of infants is included in the promise in which God declares to believers that he will be a God to them and to their seed. In this way he declared, that those deriving descent from Abraham were born to him. (Genesis 17:7) In virtue of this promise they are admitted to baptism, because they are considered members of the Church. Their salvation, therefore, has not its commencement in baptism, but being already founded on the word, is sealed by baptism. But these definitionmongers thrust forward the passage,

"Unless a man be born of water and of the Spirit."(John 3:3.)

First, assuming with them that water means baptism, who will concede to them that it moreover means a wish to receive baptism? But were I to say that the passage has a different meaning, and were I following some ancient expositors to take the term water for mortification, they would not, I presume, be so bitter as therefore to judge me heretical. I interpret it, however, as added by way of epithet to express the nature and power of the Spirit. Nor can they make out that water here means baptism, any more than that fire means some sacrament, when it is said,

"In the Holy Spirit and fire." (Matthew 3:11.)

See on what grounds they arrogate to themselves supreme authority in interpreting Scripture!

In the sixth head, they assert that we are prepared by the grace of God for receiving Justification, but they assign to this grace the office of exciting and assisting, we ourselves freely co-operating; in other words, we are here treated with the inanities which the sophists are wont to babble in the schools. But I ask, Is it the same thing to excite a will, and aid it when in itself weak, as to form a new heart in man, so as to make him willing? Let them answer, then, whether creating a new heart, and making a heart of flesh out of a heart of stone, (both of which the Scripture declares that God does in us,) is nothing else than to supply what is wanting to a weak will. But if they are not moved by these passages, let them say whether he who makes us to be willing simply assists the will. Paul claims the whole work for God; they ascribe nothing to him but a little help. But for what do they join man as an associate with God? Because man, though he might repudiate it, freely accepts the grace of God and the illumination of the Holy Spirit. How greatly do they detract from the work of God as described by the Prophet! — "I will put my law," says he, "in your hearts, and make you to walk in my precepts." Jeremiah 32:39; Ezekiel 36:27; Hebrews 8:10; 10:16.

Is this the doctrine delivered by Augustine, when he says, "Men labor to find in our will some good thing of our own not given us of God; what they can find I know not?" (Aug. Lib. de Precator. Merit. et Remiss. 2.) Indeed, as he elsewhere says, "Were man left to his own will to remain under the help of God if he chooses, while God does not make him willing, among temptations so numerous and so great, the will would succumb from its own weakness. Succor, therefore, has been brought to the weakness of the human will by divine grace acting irresistibly and inseparably, that thus the will however weak might not fail." (Aug. de Corruptione et Gratia,) But the Neptunian fathers, in a new smithy, forge what was unknown to Augustine, viz., that the reception of grace is not of God, inasmuch as it is by the free movement of our own will we assent to God calling. This is repugnant to Scripture, which makes God the author of a good will. It is one thing for the will to be moved by God to obey if it pleases, and another for it to be formed to be good. Moreover, God promises not to act so that we may be able to will well, but to make us will well. Nay, he goes farther when he says, "I will make you to walk;" as was carefully observed by Augustine. The same thing is affirmed by Paul when he teaches, that, "it is God that worketh in us both to will and to do of his good pleasure." The hallucination of these Fathers is in dreaming that we are offered a movement which leaves us an intermediate choice, while they never think of that effectual working by which the heart of man is renewed from pravity to rectitude. But this effectual working of the Holy Spirit is described in the thirty-second chapter of Jeremiah, where he thus speaks in the name of God, "I will put the fear of my name into their hearts, that they decline not from my commandments." In short, their error lies in making no distinction between the grace of Regeneration, which now comes to the succor of our wretchedness, and the first; grace which had been given to Adam. This Augustine carefully expounds. "Through Christ the Mediator," he says, "God makes those who were wicked to be good for ever after. The first man had not that grace by which he could never wish to be bad; for the help given him was of that nature that he might abandon it when he would, and remain in it if he would, but it was not such as to make him willing. The grace of the second Adam is more powerful. It makes us will, will so strongly and love so ardently, that by the will of the spirit we overcome the will of the flesh lusting against it." A little farther on he says, "Through this grace of God in receiving good and persevering therein, there is in us a power not only to be able to do what we will, but to will what we are able." (Aug. Lib. ad Bonif. 2, c. 8.) Although the subject is too long to be despatched thus briefly, I feel confident that my statement, though short, will suffice with readers of sense to refute these fancies.

But they pretend that they have also the support of Scripture. For when it is said,

"Turn thou me, O Lord, and I shall be turned," (Jeremiah 31:18,)

they infer that there is a preventing grace given to men: and, on the other hand, out of the words, "Turn ye unto me, and I will turn unto you," they extract the power of free-will. I am aware that Augustine uses this distinction, but it is in a very different sense: For he distinctly declares, and that in numerous passages, that the grace of God so works in us as to make us willing or unwilling, whence he concludes that man does no good thing which God does not do in him. (Aug. Lib. ad Bonif. 3, c. 8.) What then, you will ask, does Augustine mean when he speaks of the freedom of the will? Just what he so often repeats, that men are not forced by the grace of God against their will, but ruled voluntarily, so as to obey and follow of their own accord, and this because their will from being bad is turned to good. Hence he says, "We therefore will, but God works in us also to will. We work, but God causes us also to work." Again, "The good which we possess not without our own will we should never possess unless he worked in us also to will." Again, "It is certain that we will when we are willing, but he makes us to be willing. It is certain that we do when we do, but he makes us to do by affording most effectual strength to the will." (Aug. Lib. 2:de Bon. Persev. cap. 13; Lib. 2:23, de Graf. et Liber. Arbit.) The whole may be thus summed up — Their error consists in sharing the work between God and ourselves, so as to transfer to ourselves the obedience of a pious will in assenting to divine grace, whereas this is the proper work of God himself.

But they insist on the words of the Prophet, that in requiring conversion from us he addresses free-will, which he would do in vain (that is, in their opinion) unless free-will were something. I admit that expressions of this kind would be absurd if there were not some will in man, but I do not therefore concede that the free faculty of obeying may be thence inferred. Those venerable Fathers must be the merest of novices if they form their estimate of what man is able to do from the commandments given him, seeing that God requires of us what is above our strength for the very purpose of convincing us of our imbecility, and divesting us of all pride. Let us remember, therefore, that will in man is one thing, and the free choice of good and evil another: for freedom of choice having been taken away after the fall of the first man, will alone was left; but so completely captive under the tyranny of sin, that it is only inclined to evil.

Moreover, not to dwell longer here, I say that the doctrine here delivered by the Fathers of Trent is at open war with our Savior's words,

"Whosoever hath heard of the Father, cometh unto me." (John 6:45.)

For as Augustine wisely observes, it hence follows, that no man hears and learns of God without at the same time believing on Christ; and that the motion of the Holy Spirit is so efficacious that it always begets faith. They, on the contrary, place it in the option of man to listen to the inspiration of God, if he will! It is impossible to reconcile the two things — that all who have learned of God believe in Christ, and that the inspiration of God is not effectual and complete unless men of themselves assent to it. We have the Son of God, who is never at variance with himself, for the author of the former. To whom shall we ascribe the latter, which is utterly contrary to it, but to the father of lies?

After treating, under the seventh head, of The Mode of Preparation, so frigidly that every one but a savories Papist must feel ashamed of such senselessness, they at length, under the eighth head, when they come to define, set out with cautioning us against supposing that the justification of man consists in faith alone. The verbal question is, What is Justification? They deny that it is merely the forgiveness of sins, and insist that it includes both renovation and sanctification. Let us see whether this is true. Paul's words are,

"David describeth the blessedness of the man to whom God imputeth righteousness without works, saying, Blessed are they whose iniquities are forgiven." (Romans 4:6; Psalm 32:1.)

If, from this passage of David, Paul duly extracts a definition of gratuitous righteousness, it follows that it consists in the forgiveness of sins. Paul interprets thus — David calls him righteous to whom God imputeth righteousness by not imputing sin, and the same Apostle, without appealing to the testimony of another, elsewhere says, "God was in Christ reconciling the world unto himself, not imputing unto men their trespasses." Immediately after, he adds,

"He made him who knew no sin to be sin for us, that we might be the righteousness of God in him." (2 Corinthians 5:19.)

Can anything be clearer than that we are regarded as righteous in the sight of God, because our sins have been expiated by Christ, and no longer hold us under liability?

There is no room for the vulgar quibble that Paul is speaking of the beginning of Justification; for in both places he is showing, not how men who had hitherto been unbelievers begin to be righteous, but how they retain the righteousness which they have once procured during the whole course of life; for David speaks of himself after he had been adopted among the children of God; and Paul asserts that this is the perpetual message which is daily heard in the Church. In the same sense also he says, "Moses describeth the righteousness of the law, that he who doeth these things shall live in them, (Leviticus 18:5;) but the righteousness of faith thus speaketh, He that believeth," etc. (Romans 10:5.) We thus see that the righteousness of faith, which by no means consists of works, is opposed to the righteousness of the law, which so consists. The words have the same meaning as those which, as Luke tells us, Paul used to the people of Antioch,

"By this man is preached unto you the forgiveness of sins, and every one who believeth in him is justified from all the things from which ye could not be justified by the law of Moses." (Acts 13:38.)

For justification is added to forgiveness of sins by way of interpretation, and without doubt means acquittal. It is denied to the works of the law; and that it may be gratuitous, it is said to be obtained by faith. What! can the justification of the publican have any other meaning (Luke 17) than the imputation of righteousness, when he was freely accepted of God? And since the dispute is concerning the propriety of a word, when Christ is declared by Paul to be our righteousness and sanctification, a distinction is certainly drawn between these two things, though the Fathers of Trent confound them. For if there is a twofold grace, inasmuch as Christ both justifies and sanctifies us, righteousness does not include under it renovation of life. When it is said, "Who shall lay anything to the charge of God's elect? — It is God that justifieth" — it is impossible to understand anything else than gratuitous acceptance.

I would be unwilling to dispute about a word, did not the whole case depend upon it. But when they say that a man is justified, when he is again formed for the obedience of God, they subvert the whole argument of Paul,

"If righteousness is by the law, faith is nullified, and the promise abolished." (Romans 4:14.)

For he means, that not an individual among mankind will be found in whom the promise of salvation may be accomplished, if it involves the condition of innocence; and that faith, if it is propped up by works, will instantly fall. This is true; because, so long as we look at what we are in ourselves, we must tremble in the sight of God, so far from having a firm and unshaken confidence of eternal life. I speak of the regenerate; for how far from righteousness is that newness of life which is begun here below?

It is not to be denied, however, that the two things, Justification and Sanctification, are constantly conjoined and cohere; but from this it is erroneously inferred that they are one and the same. For example: — The light of the sun, though never unaccompanied with heat, is not to be considered heat. Where is the man so undiscerning as not to distinguish the one from the other? We acknowledge, then, that as soon as any one is justified, renewal also necessarily follows: and there is no dispute as to whether or not Christ sanctifies all whom he justifies. It were to rend the gospel, and divide Christ himself, to attempt to separate the righteousness which we obtain by faith from repentance.

The whole dispute is as to The Cause of Justification. The Fathers of Trent pretend that it is twofold, as if we were justified partly by forgiveness of sins and partly by spiritual regeneration; or, to express their view in other words, as if our righteousness were composed partly of imputation, partly of quality. I maintain that it is one, and simple, and is wholly included in the gratuitous acceptance of God. I besides hold that it is without us, because we are righteous in Christ only. Let them produce evidence from Scripture, if they have any, to convince us of their doctrine. I, while I have the whole Scripture supporting me, will now be satisfied with this one reason, viz., that when mention is made of the righteousness of works, the law and the gospel place it in the perfect obedience of the law; and as that nowhere appears, they leave us no alternative but to flee to Christ alone, that we may be regarded as righteous in him, not being so in ourselves. Will they produce to us one passage which declares that begun newness of life is approved by God as righteousness either in whole or in part? But if they are devoid of authority, why may we not be permitted to repudiate the figment of partial justification which they here obtrude?

Moreover, how frivolous and nugatory the division of causes enumerated by them is, I omit to show, except that I neither can nor ought to let pass the very great absurdity of calling Baptism alone the instrumental cause. What then will become of the gospel? Will it not even be allowed to occupy the smallest corner? But baptism is the sacrament of faith. Who denies it? Yet, when all has been said, it must still be granted me that it is nothing else than an appendage of the gospel. They, therefore, act preposterously in assigning it the first place, and act just as any one who should call a mason's trowel the instrumental cause of a house! Unquestionably, whosoever postponing the gospel enumerates baptism among the causes of salvation, by so doing gives proof that he knows not what baptism is, what its force, its office, or its use. What else I wish to say of the formal cause will be said on the tenth Canon. Here I wish only to advert to what belongs to the present place. For they again affirm that we are truly righteous, and not merely counted so. I, on the contrary, while I admit that we are never received into the favor of God without being at the same time regenerated to holiness of life, contend that it is false to say that any part of righteousness (justification) consists *in quality*, or in the habit which resides in us, and that we are righteous (justified) only by gratuitous acceptance. For when the Apostle teaches that

"by the obedience of one many were made righteous," (Romans 6:19)

he sufficiently shows, if I mistake not, that the righteousness wanting in ourselves is borrowed elsewhere. And in the first chapter to the Ephesians, where he says that we are adopted to the predestination of sons of God, that we might be accepted in the Beloved, he comprehends the whole of our righteousness. For however small the portion attributed to our work, to that extent faith will waver, and our whole salvation be endangered. Wherefore, let us learn with the Apostle to lay aside our own righteousness, which is of the law, as a noxious impediment, that we may lay hold of that which is of the faith of Jesus Christ. (Philippians 3:9.) Of what nature this is we have abundantly shown; and Paul intimates in a single sentence in the third chapter to the Galatians, that the righteousness of the law, because it consists of works, has no congruity with the righteousness of faith.

But what can you do with men like these? For after they have enumerated many causes of Justification, forgetting that they were treating of the cause of justification, they infer that righteousness partly consists of works, because no man is reconciled to God by Christ without the Spirit of regeneration. How gross the delusion! It is just as if they were to say, that forgiveness of sins cannot be disssevered from repentance, and therefore repentance is a part of it. The only point in dispute is, how we are deemed righteous in the sight of God, and where our faith, by which alone we obtain righteousness, ought to seek it? Though they should repeat a thousand times, that we cannot share in the merit of Christ's passion, without being at the same time regenerated by his Spirit, they will not make it cease to be a fundamental principle; that God is propitious to us because he was appeased by the death of Christ; and that we are counted righteous in his sight, because by that sacrifice our transgressions were expiated. "We have propitiation," says Paul, "through faith in the blood of Christ." (Romans 3:25; 5:11.) In fine, when the cause is inquired into, of what use is it to obtrude an inseparable accident? Let them cease then to sport with trifles, or trifle with quibbles such as — man receives faith, and along with it hope and love; therefore it is not faith alone that justifies. Because if eyes are given us, and along with them ears and feet and hands, we cannot therefore say that we either hear with our feet or walk with our hands, or handle with our eyes. Of the erroneous application of a passage of Paul I shall speak elsewhere.

Next follows their approbation of the worse than worthless distinction between an informal and a formed Faith. The venerable Fathers, indeed, are ashamed to use the very terms, but while they stammer out that man is not united to Christ by faith alone, unless hope and charity are added, they are certainly dreaming of that faith, devoid of charity, which is commonly called by the sophists informal. They thus betray their gross incapacity. For if the doctrine of Paul is true, that

"Christ dwells in our hearts by faith," (Ephesians 3:17)

they can no more separate faith from charity than Christ from his Spirit. If "our hearts are purified by faith," as Peter affirms, (Acts 15:9,) if "whosoever believeth hath eternal life," as our Savior so often declares, (John 3:16; 5:24; 6:40; 20:31,) if the inheritance of eternal life is obtained by faith, (Romans 5:14,) faith is something very different from all forms of dead persuasion. They deny that we are made living members of Christ by faith. How much better Augustine, who calls faith the life of the soul, as the soul is the life of the body? (Aug. in Joan. c. 11,) although Augustine is not so much the authority to be quoted here as Paul, who acknowledges that he lives by the faith of Christ. (Galatians 2:20.) They should perhaps be pardoned this error, because they talk about faith as they might do of fabulous islands, (for who among them knows by the slightest experience what faith is?) were it not that they drag the miserable world along with them in the same ignorance to destruction!

Let us remember that the nature of Faith is to be estimated from Christ. For that which God offers to us in Christ we receive only by faith. Hence, whatever Christ is to us is transferred to faith, which makes us capable of receiving both Christ and all his blessings. There would be no truth in the words of John, that faith is the victory by which we overcome the world, (1 John 5:4,) did it not ingraft us into Christ, (John 16:33,) who is the only conqueror of the world. It is worth while to remark their stupidity. When they quote the passage of Paul,

"Faith which worketh by love," (Galatians 5:6)

they do not see that they are cutting their own throats. For if love is the fruit and effect of faith, who sees not that the informal faith which they have fabricated is a vain figment? It is very odd for the daughter thus to kill the mother! But I must remind my readers that that passage is irrelevantly introduced into a question about Justification, since Paul is not there considering in what respect faith or charity avails to justify a man, but what is Christian perfection; as when he elsewhere says,

"If a man be in Christ he is a new creature." (2 Corinthians 5:17)

It were long and troublesome to note every blunder, but there is one too important to be omitted. They add, "that when catechumens ask faith from the Church, the answer is, "If you will enter into life, keep the commandments.'" (Matthew 19:17.) Wo to their catechumens, if so hard a condition is laid upon them! For what else is this but to lay them under an eternal curse, since they acknowledge with Paul, that all are under the curse who are subject to the law? (Galatians 3:10.) But they have the authority of Christ! I wish they would observe to what intent Christ thus spake. This can only be ascertained from the context, and the character of the persons. He to whom Christ replies had asked, What must I do to have eternal life? Assuredly, whosoever wishes to merit life by works, has a rule prescribed to him by the law, "This do, and thou shalt live." But attention must be paid to the object of this as intimated by Paul, viz., that man experiencing his powers, or rather convinced of his powerlessness, may lay aside his pride, and flee all naked to Christ. There is no room for the righteousness of faith until we have discovered that it is in vain that salvation is promised us by the law. But that which the law could not do in that it was weak through the flesh, God performed by his own Son, by expiating our sins through the sacrifice of his death, so that his righteousness is fulfilled in us. But so preposterous are the Fathers of Trent, that while it is the office of Moses to lead us by the hand to Christ, (Galatians 3:24,) they lead us away from the grace of Christ to Moses.

Lest they should not be liberal enough in preaching up the powers of man, they again repeat, under this head, that the Spirit of God acts in us according to the proper disposedness and co-operation of each. What disposedness, pray, will the Spirit of God find in stony hearts? Are they not ashamed to feign a disposedness, when the Spirit himself uniformly declares in Scripture that all things are contrary? For the commencement of grace is to make those willing who were unwilling, and therefore repugnant; so that faith, as well in its beginnings as its increase, even to its final perfection, is the gift of God; and the preparation for receiving grace is the free election of God, as Augustine says, (Lib. 1:de Praedest., Sanct. c. 9-11.) And the words of Paul are clear,

"God hath blessed us with all spiritual blessings, according as he hath chosen us in Christ, according to the good pleasure of his will." (Ephesians 1:3.)

By these words he certainly restrains us, while receiving so great a blessing from God, from glorying in the decision of our will, as Augustine again says. (Ibid. c. 8.) This which man ought to receive as at the hands of God, is he to oppose to him as a merit of his own? For whence is there a first disposition, unless because we are the sheep of Christ! And who dare presume so far as to say he makes himself a sheep? Accordingly, when Luke speaks of effectual calling, he tells us that not those who were disposed of themselves, but those who were pre-ordained to eternal life, believed. (Acts 13:48.) And Paul acquaints us whence a right disposition is, when he teaches that the good works in which we walk were prepared by God. (Ephesians 2:10.) Let us hear Augustine, whose doctrine is very different, rather than those babblers. "After the fall of man," he says, (Lib. 2: de Bono Persev., c. 9,) "God was pleased that man's approach to him should be the effect only of his grace, and that man's not withdrawing from him should also be the effect only of his grace." For it is he himself who promises that he will give us a heart that we may understand, and ears that we may hear. Wherefore it is His grace alone which makes the difference, as Paul reminds us. Let me conclude by again using the words of Augustine, "The human will obtains not grace by freedom, but freedom by grace, and in order that it may persevere, delectable perpetuity and insuperable fortitude," (Lib. de Corrupt. et Grat. c. 8.)

In the ninth chapter, while they desire to show some signs of modesty, they rather betray their effrontery. Seeing that the doctrine of Scripture was obviously repugnant to their decrees, they, to prevent this from being suspected, first explain what it is for a man to be justified by faith, saying, that faith is the beginning of salvation, and the foundation of justification. As if they had disentangled themselves by this solution, they immediately fly off to another — that the Apostle teaches that we are justified freely, because all the things which precede justification, whether faith or works, do not merit it. Did they think they are engaged in a serious matter, would they perform it as giddily as if they were playing at see-saw? I say nothing of their disregard of the judgments of mankind, as if they had expected to put out the eyes of all by such a sacred dogma as this — Faith justifies, since it begins justification. First, this comment is repugnant to common sense. For what can be more childish than to restrict the whole effect to the mere act of beginning?

But let us see for a little whether the words of Paul allow themselves to be so easily wrested. "The gospel," he says, (Romans 1:16) "is the, power of God to every one believing unto salvation; for therein is the righteousness of God revealed from faith to faith." Who sees not that here the beginning and the end are alike included? Were it otherwise, it would have been said, from "faith to works," as they would finish what faith begins. To the same effect is the testimony of Habakkuk, "The just shall live by fairly." (Habakkuk 2:4.) This would be improperly said did not faith perpetuate life. In the person of Abraham the chief mirror of justification is held forth. Let us see, then, at what time faith is declared to have been imputed to him for righteousness. (Genesis 15:6; Galatians 3:6.) He was certainly not a novice, but having left his country, had for several years followed the Lord, so that he was no common exemplar of holiness and all virtue. Faith therefore does not open up an access to him to righteousness, in order that his justification may afterwards be completed elsewhere. And Paul at length concludes that we stand in the grace which we have obtained by faith. (Romans 5:2.) As far as a fixed and immovable station is from a transient passage, so far are they in this dogma of theirs from the meaning of Paul. To collect all the passages of Scripture were tedious and superfluous. From these few, I presume, it is already super-abundantly clear, that the completion, not less than the commencement of justification, must be ascribed to faith.

The second branch is, that Justification is said by Paul to be gratuitous, because no merit precedes it. What then? When Paul also exclaims that all glorying of the flesh is excluded by the law of faith, is he looking only to the merits of past life, and does he not rather remind us that men justified by faith have nothing in which they can glory to the very end of life? For when he asserts after David that righteousness is imputed without works, he declares what is the perpetual state of believers. (Romans 3:27; 4:2.) In like manner David exclaims, that himself and all the other children of God are blessed by the remission of sins, not for one day, but for the whole of life. (Psalm 32:1.) Nor does Peter, in the Acts, speak of the justification of a single day, when he says,

"We believe that through the grace of Jesus Christ we are saved, as did also our fathers." (Acts 15:11.)

The question under discussion was, whether observance of the law was to be exacted of the Gentiles. He says it ought not, because there is no other salvation in the Christian Church than through the grace of Christ, and there never was any other. (Acts 4:12.) And justly; for, as Paul says, the promise will not be secure unless it depends on the grace of God and on faith. (Romans 4:16.) Will they pretend that he is here, too, speaking of preceding merits? Nay, he declares that the greatest saints can have no assurance of salvation, unless it repose on the grace of Christ. He therefore abolishes faith who does not retain his as the only righteousness, which exists even until death.

We are justified freely, they say, because no works which precede justification merit it. But when Paul takes away all ground of glorying from Abraham, on the ground that faith was imputed to him for righteousness, he immediately subjoins by way of proof — where works are, there a due reward is paid, whereas what is given to faith is gratuitous. Let us observe that he is, speaking of the holy Patriarch. Paul affirms, that at the time when he renounced the world to devote himself entirely to God, he was not justified by any works. If these spurious Fathers object, that it was then only he began to be justified, the quibble is plainly refuted by the context of the Sacred History. He had for many years exercised himself in daily prayer to God, and he had constantly followed the call of God, wherein was contained the promise of eternal life. Must they not therefore be thrice blind who see no gratuitous righteousness of God, except in the very vestibule, and think that the merit of works pervades the edifice? But it is proper to attend to the gloss by which they attempt to cloak this gross impiety, viz., that in this way they satisfy the Apostle's sentiment,

"If it be of grace, then it is no more of works." (Romans 11:5)

But Paul ascribes it to Divine grace that a remnant is left, and that they are miraculously preserved by God from the danger of eternal destruction, even unto the end. Far, therefore, is he from restricting it to so small a portion, i.e., to the beginning alone.

It was indeed an absurd dream, but they are still more grossly absurd when they give it as their opinion, that none of all the things which precede Justification, whether faith or works, merit it. What works antecedent to Justification are they here imagining? What kind of order is this in which the fruit is antecedent in time to the root? In one word, that pious readers may understand how great progress has been made in securing purity of doctrine, the monks dunned into the ears of the reverend Fathers, whose part was to nod assent, this old song, that good works which precede justification are not meritorious of eternal salvation, but preparatory only. If any works precede faith, they should also be taken into account. But there is no merit, because there are no works; for if men inquire into their works, they will find only evil works.

Posterity will scarcely believe that the Papacy had fallen into such a stupor as to imagine the possibility of any work antecedent to justification, even though they denied it to be meritorious of so great a blessing! For what can come from man until he is born again by the Spirit of God? Very different is the reasoning of Paul. He exhorts the Ephesians to remember (Ephesians 2) that they were saved by grace, not by themselves nor by their own works. He subjoins a proof, not the one which these insane Fathers use, that no works which precede suffice, but the one which I have adduced, that we are possessed of no works but those which God hath prepared, because we are his workmanship created unto a holy and pious life. Faith, moreover, precedes justification, but in such a sense, that in respect of God, it follows. What they say of faith might perhaps hold true, were faith itself, which puts us in possession of righteousness, our own. But seeing that it too is the free gift of God, the exception which they introduce is superfluous. Scripture, indeed, removes all doubt on another ground, when it opposes faith to works, to prevent its being classed among merits. Faith brings nothing of our own to God, but receives what God spontaneously offers us. Hence it is that faith, however imperfect, nevertheless possesses a perfect righteousness, because it has respect to nothing but the gratuitous goodness of God.

In the tenth chapter, they inveigh against what they call The Vain Confidence of Heretics. This consists, according to their definition, in our holding it as certain that our sins are forgiven, and resting in this certainty. But if such certainty makes heretics, where will be the happiness which David extols? (Psalm 32) Nay, where will be the peace of which Paul discourses in the fifth chapter to the Romans, if we rest in anything but the good-will of God? How, moreover, have we God propitious, but just because he enters not into judgment with us? They acknowledge that sins are never forgiven for Christ's sake, except freely, but leaving it in suspense to whom and when they are forgiven, they rob all consciences of calm placid confidence. Where, then, is that boldness of which Paul elsewhere speaks, (Ephesians 3:12,) that access with confidence to the

Father through faith in Christ? Not contented with the term confidence, he furnishes us with boldness, which is certainly something more than certainty. And what shall we say to his own occasional use of the term certainty? (Romans 8:37.) This certainty he founds upon nothing but a mere persuasion of the free love of God. Nay, they overthrow all true prayer to God, when they keep pious minds suspended by fear which alone shuts the door of access against us. "He who doubts," says James, (James 1:6) "is like a wave of the sea driven by the wind." Let not such think that they shall obtain anything of the Lord. "Let him who would pray effectually not doubt." Attend to the antithesis between faith and doubt, plainly intimating that faith is destroyed as soon as certainty is taken away.

But that the whole of their theology may be more manifest to my readers, let them weigh the words which follow under the same head. It ought not to be asserted, they say, that those who have been truly justified ought to entertain an unhesitating doubt that they are justified. If it be so, let them teach how plhroforia (full assurance) can be reconciled with doubt. For Paul makes it the perpetual attendant of faith. I say nothing as to their laying down as a kind of axiom what Paul regards as a monstrous absurdity. "If the inheritance is by the law," he says, (Romans 4:14,) "faith is made void." He argues that there will be no certainty of faith if it depends on human works — a dependence which he hesitates not to pronounce most absurd. And justly; seeing he immediately infers from it that the promise also is abolished.

I am ashamed to debate the matter, as if it were doubtful, with men who call themselves Christians. The doctrine of Scripture is clear. "We know," says John, (1 John 4:6,) "that we are the children of God." And he afterwards explains whence this knowledge arises, viz., from the Spirit which he hath given us. In like manner Paul, too, reminds us, (1

Corinthians 2:12) "That we have not received the spirit of the world but the Spirit which is of God, that we may know the things which are given us of God." Elsewhere it is said still more explicitly, "We have not received the spirit of bondage again to fear, but the Spirit of adoption, whereby we cry, Abba, Father." (Romans 8:15.) Hence that access with confidence and boldness which we mentioned a little ago. And, indeed, they are ignorant of the whole nature of faith who mingle doubt with it. Were Paul in doubt, he would not exult over death, and write as he does in the eighth of the Romans, when he boasts of being so certain of the love of God that nothing can turn him from the persuasion. This is clear from his words. And he assigns the cause, "Because the love of God is shed abroad in our hearts by the Holy Spirit which is given to us." By this he intimates that our conscience, resting in the testimony of the Holy Spirit, boldly glories in the presence of God, in the hope of eternal life. But it is not strange that this certainty, which the Spirit of God seals on the hearts of the godly, is unknown to sophists. Our Savior foretold that so it would be.

"Not the world, but you alone in whom he abideth, will know him." (John 14:17.)

It is not strange that those who, having discarded the foundation of faith, lean rather on their works, should waver to and fro. For it is a most true saying of Augustine, (in Psalm 88,) "As the promise is sure, not according to our merits, but according to his grace, no man ought to speak with trepidation of that of which he cannot doubt."

They think, however, that they ingeniously obviate all objections when they recommend a general persuasion of the grace of Christ. They prohibit any doubt as to the efficacy of Christ's death. But where do they wish it to be placed In the air, so as to be only in confused imagination. For they allow none to apply grace to themselves with the firm assurance of faith, as if we had to no purpose received such promises as these, "Behold your king cometh;" "Ye are the heirs of promise;" "The Father is pleased in thee;" "The righteousness of God is unto all and upon all them that believe." (Matthew 21:5; Zechariah 9:9; Acts 2:39; Luke 12:32; Romans 3:22.) Surely, if they admit that by faith we apprehend what God offers to us, Christ is not set before me and others, merely that we may believe him to have been the Redeemer of Abraham, but that every one may appropriate the salvation which he procured. And how improper is it to assert that "no man can know with certainty of faith that he has obtained the grace of God." Paul and John recognize none as the children of God but those who know it. Of what knowledge can we understand them to speak, but that which they have learned by the teaching of the Holy Spirit? Admirably says Bernard, (Sermon 5 in Dedicat. Temp.,) "Faith must here come to our aid; here truth must lend us succor; that that which lies hid in the heart of the Father respecting us may be revealed by the Spirit, or the Spirit may persuade our hearts that we are the children of God; and persuade by calling and justifying us freely by faith." But if Paul, when he exhorts the Corinthians to prove themselves whether they be in the faith, (2 Corinthians 13:5,) pronounces all reprobate who do not know Christ dwelling in them, why should I hesitate to pronounce them twice reprobate, who, not allowing the Church to enter on any such proof, abolish all certainty concerning the grace of God?

Under the eleventh, head, when they describe Increase of Righteousness, they not only confound the free imputation of righteousness with the merit of works, but almost exterminate it. Their words are, "Believers increase in righteousness by good works, through the observance of the commandments of God and the Church, and are thence more justified." They ought at least to use the exception of Augustine. (De Civit. 19 c.

27.) "The righteousness of believers, while they live in the world, consists more in the forgiveness of sins than the perfection of virtues." He teaches that no dependence at all is to be placed on righteousness of works, which he names with contempt. For he declares that the only hope of all the godly who groan under the weakness of the flesh is, that they have a mediator, Christ Jesus, who is the propitiation for their sins. (Lib. ad Bonif., 5 c. 5.) On the contrary, the Fathers of Trent; or rather the hireling monks, who, as a kind of Latin pipers, compose for them whatever tune they please, doing their utmost to call their disciples away from the view of grace, blind them by a false confidence in works. We, indeed, willingly acknowledge, that believers ought to make daily increase in good works, and that the good works wherewith they are adorned by God, are sometimes distinguished by the name of righteousness. But since the whole value of works is derived from no other fountain than that of gratuitous acceptance, how absurd were it to make the former overthrow the latter! Why do they not remember what they learned when boys at school, that what is subordinate is not contrary? I say that it is owing to free imputation that we are considered righteous before God; I say that from this also another benefit proceeds, viz., that our works have the name of righteousness, though they are far from having the reality of righteousness. In short, I affirm, that not by our own merit but by faith alone, are both our persons and works justified; and that the justification of works depends on the justification of the person, as the effect on the cause. Therefore, it is necessary that the righteousness of faith alone so precede in order, and be so pre-eminent in degree, that nothing can go before it or obscure it.

Hence it is a most iniquitous perversion to substitute some kind of meritorious for a gratuitous righteousness, as if God after justifying us once freely in a single moment, left us to procure righteousness for ourselves by the observance of the law during the whole of life. As to the observance of the Divine Commandments, they must, whether they will or not, confess this much, that all mortals are very far from accomplishing it perfectly. Let them now answer, and say whether any part of it whatever be righteousness, or a part of righteousness? They will strenuously maintain the latter. But it is repugnant to Scripture, which gives this honor to none but perfect obedience. "The man who doeth these things shall live in them;"

"Cursed is he that continueth not in all things written in the book of the law to do them." (Galatians 3:10.)

Again,

"He who fails in one point is guilty of all." (James 2:10.)

There is no man who does not acknowledge, without one word from me, that we are all subject to the curse while we keep halting at the observance of the law, and that righteousness, since works cannot procure it, must be borrowed from some other quarter of the commandments of the Church, which they mix up with those of God, we shall speak elsewhere. My readers, however, must be informed in passing, that no kind of impiety is here omitted. Who can excuse their profanity in not hesitating to claim a power of justifying for their own inventions? Never did even Pelagius attempt this. He attempted to fascinate miserable men by the impious persuasion that they could, by the observance of the Divine law, acquire righteousness for themselves; but to attribute this merit to human laws never entered his mind. It is execrable blasphemy against God for any mortal to give way to such presumption as to award eternal life to the observance of his own traditions.

But whither shall I turn? It is a Sacred Council that speaks, and it cannot err in the interpretation of Scripture. And they have passages of Scripture, the first out of Ecclesiasticus, "Fear not to be justified even until death." I believe there is one way of getting myself out of the difficulty. Let my readers look at the passage, and they will find that the worthy Fathers have impudently corrupted it; for the writer says, "Be not forbidden, i.e., prevented until death," although it ought rather to be rendered defer not; for this the Greek word means. He is inveighing against the slothfulness of those who put off their conversion to God. What was thus spoken of the commencement, these religious Fathers, not only in gross ignorance, but open malice, apply to progress. In the passage of James there is more plausibility. (James 2:24.) But any one who has read our writings knows well enough that James gives them no support, inasmuch as he uses justification to signify, not the cause of righteousness, but the proof of it. This plainly appears from the context. But they become more ridiculous when they infer that a man is justified by good works because the Church prays for increase of faith, hope, and charity. Who, if he is not too old to be a child, is not frightened at this thunder?

Under the twelfth head they renew the old anathema: Let none say that the Commandments of God are impossible to be observed by a justified man. It serves no purpose to dispute about the term impossible. It is enough for me, and should be enough for all who are pious, and not at all contentious, that no man ever lived who satisfied the law of God, and that none ever can be found. What! shall we accuse the Holy Spirit of falsehood, when he charges all men with the guilt of transgression, not those of our age only, but all who shall ever exist to the end of the world? "There is not a man upon earth," saith Solomon, "who sinneth not." (1 Kings 8:46.) And David had said,

"In thy sight shall no man living be justified." (Psalm 143:2.)

If it be possible to find any one who can fulfill the law, let the Holy Spirit retract. But far from us be the devilish pride of making the eternal Author of truth a liar. Nay, even Paul's argument would fail:

"It is written, Cursed is every one that continueth not in all things written in the book of the law. Therefore, whosoever are under the law are under curse." (Galatians 3:10.)

It will be easy to object, that the law can be fulfilled. But the Apostle assumes as an acknowledged principle what these men stigmatize with anathema. Accordingly in another place, when deploring the bondage in which himself, in common with all saints, was held, he could find no other remedy than that of being freed from the body. (Romans 7:24.)

The Pelagians annoyed Augustine with the same quibble. He admits that God may, if he pleases, raise men to this pitch of perfection, but that he never had, and never would, because the Scriptures teach otherwise. I go farther, and assert, that what the Scriptures declare never shall be, is impossible; although, if we are to debate about a word, the very thing was expressed by Peter, (Acts 15.) when he spoke of the yoke of the law as that which none of their fathers could bear. It is an error to suppose that this refers only to ceremonies: for what so very arduous was there in ceremonies as to make all human strength fail under the burden of them? He undoubtedly means that all mankind from the beginning were, and still are, unequal to the observance of the law, and that therefore nothing remains but to flee to the grace of Christ, which, loosing us from the yoke of the law, keeps us as it were under free custody. And it is to be observed that he is speaking of the regenerate, lest the Fathers of Trent quibble, and say that he spoke of the weakness of the flesh when the assistance of the Spirit is wanting. For he affirms that prophets and patriarchs, and pious kings, however aided by the Spirit of God, were unable to bear the yoke of the law, and declares, without ambiguity, that the observance of the law was impossible.

But they also produce Scripture as a witness on the other side: for John says, that "his commandments are not grievous." (1 John 5:3.) I admit it, provided you exclude not the doctrine of the remission of sins, which he places before all the commandments. If it be not grievous to perform the law, you will find me several men without sin to make God a liar; as is said also by John. (1 John 1:8.) But these fools consider not that the facility of which John speaks depends on this, that the saints have a remedy in readiness to supply their defects — they flee for pardon. Hence, too, it is that Christ's yoke is easy and his burden light, because the saints feel an alacrity in their liberty while they feel themselves no longer under the law. Paul applies to them this best stimulus of exhortation. (Romans 6:12.) And David also teaches,

"With thee is forgiveness, that thou mayest be feared." (Psalm 130:4.)

Take that hope of pardon from me, and the least commandment of the law will be a heavier load than Aetna. But what is this to idle monks, who have here touched with the little finger that observance of the commandments of the facility of which they so confidently prattle. Nay, they openly betray their irreligion by this one dogma. How? This admirable Apostle laments that he is held captive from inability to obey the law as is meet, and he cries out that the disease cannot be cured till death cure it. (Romans 7:23.) These sturdy doctors superdiously smile, and sing out that such complaints are causeless, because Christ's burden is light. They afterwards add,

"The disciples of Christ love him, and those who love him do his commandments." (John 14:23.)

This is all true. But where is the perfect love of Christ — love, I mean, with the whole heart, and mind, and strength? There only where the flesh lusteth not against the spirit, and therefore not in the world at all. The disciples of Christ love him with sincere and earnest affection of heart, and according to the measure of their love keep his commandments. But how small is this compared with that strict perfection in which there is no deficiency?

Let readers of sense now attend to the consistency of the *dicta* of these Fathers. After boldly asserting that the Law can be fulfilled by believers, they admit that even the most holy sometimes fall into light and daily sins. First I ask, whether there be any sin, however light, that is not inconsistent with the observance of the law? For what vicious thought will creep into the mind of man if it be wholly occupied with the love of God? The law is not satisfied unless God is loved with the whole heart. That men do not therefore cease to be righteous I admit. But why so, but just because they are blessed to whom sin is not imputed? If they insist on being righteous by works, on which their consciences can repose in the sight of God, they, in the first place, subvert faith, and do an insufferable wrong to the grace of God; and, in the second place, they bring no support to their impious doctrine as to possible observance of the law. If they consider what they call lighter lapses as nothing, the dreadful sentence of the Supreme Judge thunders forth, "He who shall despise one of these least commandments shall be called the least in the kingdom of heaven." Although I should like to know what sins they call light, (for so they speak by way of extenuation,) and why they say that the righteous fall into them sometimes rather than constantly, or ever and anon; for scarcely a moment passes in which we do not contract some new guilt. In their eyes all kinds of concupiscence which prompt us to evil are light sins, and also all kinds of temptations which urge us to blasphemy against God. Be this as it may, they are here placed in a manifest dilemma.

What afterwards follows under the same head is no more applicable than if one were to attempt to prove from the movement of the feet that the hands do not feel. They gather some exhortations to a pious life. What, pray, will they force out of these except what may be learned a hundred times better, and with very different effect, from our writings and discourses, and even daily conversation, viz., that "we are not called to uncleanness but to holiness," that "the mercy of God hath appeared, that denying the lusts of the flesh, we may live piously and holily in the world," that "we have risen with Christ to set our affections on things above:" (1 Thessalonians 4:7; Titus 2:11; Colossians 3:12.) But they seem to think they have done some great thing when they infer that it is in vain for those who are unwilling to be partakers of the sufferings of Christ, to glory in the heavenly inheritance. How much better we explain the matter let our readers judge. There is one difference, however: we teach that we are to share in the sufferings of Christ in order that we may attain to the fellowship of his blessed resurrection; (Romans 8:17;) we do not separate Christ from himself. They erroneously infer what does not at all follow — that men by suffering merit eternal life, and that part of their righteousness consisting therein, they do not depend entirely on the grace of God.

But they are still more absurd in their conclusion. For they infer that all are enemies to the Christian religion who teach that the righteous sin in every good work, at least venially. I should like to know what logic taught them to draw such an inference as this: "So run that you may obtain the reward" — ergo, In the good works of saints there is nothing that deserves blame. Must not men be thrice stupid when such fellows can persuade them that such follies proceeded from the Holy Spirit? But, passing this absurdity, let us look at the substance.

They must of necessity admit that works are to be judged from the internal affection of mind from which they emanate, and the end at which they aim, rather than from the external mask under which they appear to men: for God looketh on the heart, as was said to Samuel, and his eyes behold the truth, as Jeremiah reminds us. It is too plain, however, that we are never animated and actuated by a perfect love to God in obeying His just commands. Various passions withdraw us from our course, so that we scarcely walk when God enjoins us to hasten on with the greatest speed; we are scarcely lukewarm when we ought to be all ardor. Though from self-deception we are not sensible of this defect, God sees and judges: in his sight the stars are dim, and the sun shineth not. In short, the seventh chapter of the Romans disposes of this controversy. There Paul, in his own person and that of all the godly, confesses that he is far from perfection, even when his will is at its best. Wherefore let a man flatter himself as he may, the best work that ever was, if brought by God to judgment, will be found stained by some blemish. But these works are approved by God. Who denies it? We only maintain that they cannot please without pardon. But what is it that God pardons except sin? Hence it follows that there is nothing so very censurable in saying, that all good works whatever, if judged with strict rigor, are more deserving of eternal damnation than of the reward of life; for wherever sin, in however slight a degree, is found, no man of sound judgment will deny that there too the materials of death are found. Owing, however, to the boundless mercy of God, works have a recompense in heaven, though, they not only merited nothing of the kind, but would have the reward of eternal death were not the impurity with which they are otherwise defiled wiped away by Christ. I have moreover shown in many places how absurd the reasoning is which infers dignity or merit from the use of the term reward. The reason is obvious. The very recompense which the sophists assert to be founded on merit, depends on gratuitous acceptance.

Under the thirteenth head. if they only did what the title professes, I would give them my subscription. But since, while professing to obviate rashness and presumption, they make it their whole study to efface from the minds of the pious all confidence in their election, I am forced to oppose them, because they are plainly opposed by Scripture. For to what end does Paul discourse at such length in the first chapter to the Ephesians, on the eternal election of God, unless to persuade them that they were chosen by it unto eternal life? And there is no need of conjecture; for he repeatedly enjoins the Ephesians to hold it fixed in their minds, that they have been called and made partakers of the gospel, because they were elected in Christ before the foundation of the world. Likewise in the eighth chapter to the Romans, he expressly conjoins the doctrine of election with the assurance of faith.

I acknowledge, indeed, and we are all careful to teach, that nothing is more pernicious than to inquire into the secret council of God, with the view of thereby obtaining a knowledge of our election — that this is a whirlpool in which we shall be swallowed up stud lost. But seeing that our Heavenly Father holds forth in Christ a mirror of our eternal adoption, no man truly holds what has been given us by Christ save he who feels assured that Christ himself has been given him by the Father, that he may not perish. What! are the following passages mere verbiage? "The Father who has placed us under the protection and faith of his Son is greater than all." "The Son will not allow anything to be lost." (John 6:39; 10:28.) These things are said that all who are the sons of God may trust in such a guardian of their salvation, and feel safe in the midst of danger; nay, when beset with infinite perils, may trust that their salvation is secure because in the hand of God.

But they affirm, that it is impossible to know whom God has chosen except by special revelation. I admit it. And, accordingly, Paul says that we have not received the spirit of this world, but the Spirit which is of God, that we may know the things which are given us of God. The gift he elsewhere interprets as meaning the adoption, by which we are classed among his children, and which he holds to be so certain that we may with loud voice glory in it. But I am not unaware of what they intend by special revelation. I, however, mean that which our Heavenly Father specially deigns to bestow on his own children. Nor is this any fancy of my own.

The words of Paul are well known, "Those things which are hidden from human sense God hath revealed unto us by his Spirit, who also searcheth the deepest things of God." Again, "Who hath known the mind of God, or who hath been his counselor? But we have the mind of Christ."

On the whole, then, we see that what the venerable Fathers call rash and damnable presumption, is nothing but that holy confidence in our adoption revealed unto us by Christ, to which God everywhere encourages his people.

Under the fourteenth head they prohibit any one from feeling absolutely certain that God will bestow upon him the gift of Final Perseverance, and yet they do not disapprove of entertaining the strongest hope of it in God. But let them first show us by what kind of cement they can glue together things so opposed to each other as the strongest hope and a doubtful expectation. For certainly, he whose expectation of eternal life is not founded on absolute certainty, must be agitated by various, doubts. This is not the kind of hope which Paul describes, when he says that he is certainly persuaded that neither life nor death, nor things present, nor things to come, will dissolve the love with which God embraces him in

Christ. He would not speak thus did not the certainty of Christian hope reach beyond the last hour of life. And what language do the promises speak? The Spirit not only declares that the just lives by faith, but that he shall live. (Habakkuk 2:4.) Thus far must hope reach. Paul even shows this when he describes hope as patiently waiting for things which are yet concealed.

But, it may be said, they do not take away hope, but only absolute certainty. What! is there any expression of doubt or uncertainty when Paul boldly asserts that a crown of righteousness is laid up for him? (1 Timothy 4:8.) Is there anything conditional in the words, when he declares that an earnest of our adoption has been given us, so that we can dare with loud voice to call God our Father? They take refuge in the frivolous quibble out of which I have already driven them, viz., that Paul had this by special revelation. But he claims nothing so special for himself as not to share it with all believers, when in their name as much as his own, he boldly exults over death and life, the present and the future. Nor does John claim for himself alone that knowledge in which he glories, when he says,

"We know that we shall be like God, for we shall see him as he is." (1 John 3:2.)

Nor Paul, when he says, "We glory in hope of the glory of God;" and again, "We know that when this earthly tabernacle falls, a mansion is prepared for us in heaven." (Romans 5:2; 2 Corinthians 5:1.)

They make a gloss of what is said in the tenth chapter of First Corinthians, "Let him who standeth take heed lest he fall." Of this there is a twofold solution. Paul there only checks carnal arrogance, which has nothing to do with the assurance of hope; nor does he address believers only, but all of the Gentiles who had assumed the name of Christ, among whom there might be many puffed up with vain confidence. For the comparison which is there made between Jews and Gentiles, is not confined to the elect only, but comprehends all who belonged to the Church by name. I will be satisfied, however, with this one reply, as it is quite sufficient, viz., that the fear enjoined is not that which in the smallest degree impairs the certainty of faith or hope, but only that which keeps us solicitous in the fear of God.

The regenerate are not yet in glory, but only in the hope of glory, and much of the contest still remains. Hence did they infer that torpor must be shaken off, and no overweening security indulged, there is no man of sense who would not subscribe to them. But when they employ the passage as a battering-ram to shake the firmness of our hope, and drive us headlong, their conduct is on no account to be tolerated. In qualifying Paul's sentiment, and making it mean that the work of salvation which God has begun will be perfected in us only if we are not wanting to his grace, they act very ignorantly, not observing that one part of grace consists in having God present with us so as to prevent our being wanting to his grace. This doctrine ought not to give occasion to sloth; it ought only to make them recognize what they have received of God, and what they expect from him.

I could like, if I durst, to pass many things without affixing a stigma to them. But what can I do? There is scarcely one line which does not contain some notable error or give indications of dishonest dealing. On the fifteenth head, where they treat of recovery after the fall, they say that Jerome gave an appropriate definition of repentance, when he called it the second plank after shipwreck. Were I disposed to criticize the *dictum* of Jerome, I would ask why he calls it the second plank, and not the third or fourth? for how few are there who do not during life make more than one shipwreck. Nay: what man was ever found whom the grace of

God has not rescued from daily shipwrecks? But I have no business with Jerome at present.

The Fathers of Trent do not treat of Repentance, but of the Sacrament of Penitence, which they pretend to have been instituted by Christ. When? When he said, Receive ye the Holy Spirit; whose sins ye remit, they shall be remitted. (John 20:22.) First, because Christ gave the Apostles this authority, is it therefore a sacrament? Where is the sign? where the form? Secondly, who knows not that this office was assigned to the Apostles that they might perform it towards strangers? How asinine the Fathers must be to allow the absurd trifling of a dreaming monk thus to pass without opposition! Christ confirms the testimony which the Apostles were to bear to the world concerning the remission of sins. Such is the message which is conveyed by the gospel, and that, too, 'Lo those who are not yet chosen into the Church. Some babbler among the monks who rule the Council having never perhaps looked at the passage, certainly never pondered it, read out his own commentary that there a formula is prescribed by which those who had fallen after baptism were to be restored to a state of grace. The stupid Fathers nodded assent. The passage itself, however, proclaims that it was Shamelessly wrested. They infer that the penitence of a Christian man after a lapse, is very different from baptismal penitence: as if Christ had only referred to one species, and not expressly required, as the twenty-fourth chapter of Luke informs us, that repentance as well as remission of sins should be preached in his name.

They go farther, and say, that this Penitence with which they trifle consists not only in contrition of heart, but the confession of the mouth and the satisfaction of works: although not to appear unmerciful, they mitigate the rigor of their law when they allow' themselves to be appeased by a wish to confess. Why should I begin a long discussion here? The point is the remission of sins: which is the knowledge of salvation. (Luke 1:77.) God promises it to us free in the blood, of Christ: of auricular confession he says not a word. These new lawgivers tie down forgiveness to a formula of confession, contrary to the command of God, and assert that it is redeemed by satisfaction. What will remain for miserable consciences, if they are forced to abandon the word of God and acquiesce in the decrees of men?

I am desirous to be assured of my salvation. I am shown in the word of God a simple way, which will lead me straight to the entire and tranquil possession of this great boon. I will say no more. Men come and lay hands on me, and tie me down to a necessity of confession from which Christ frees me. They lay upon me the burden of satisfaction, ordering me to provide at my own hand that which Christ shows me is to be sought from his blood alone. Can I long doubt what it is expedient to do? Nay, away with all hesitation, when attempts are made to lead us away from the only author of our salvation. Search as they may, not a syllable will be found by which Christ orders us to confess our sins into a human ear. All the promises relating to the remission of sins make not the smallest mention of such a thing. The law was wholly unknown to the Apostles. Throughout the Eastern Church it was scarcely ever used. Nay, the observance was everywhere free for more than a thousand years, till Innocent III., with a few of his horned crew, entangled the Christian people in this net, which the Fathers of Trent would now make fast;. What I say is abundantly testified by ancient history. Our books are filled with proofs. None of them are unknown to those who dictated this famous formula to the Council; and yet so impudent are they, that they would persuade us by one word that the door of salvation is closed, and can only be opened by the key of a fictitious confession. But who will grant them a license to restrict the promises of Christ, by imposing any condition they please?

I do not say at present how cruel an executioner to torture and excruciate consciences is that law of Innocent which they anew promulgate; how many it has driven headlong to despair; what a narcotic of hypocrisy it has been to lull others asleep; how many monstrous iniquities have sprung from it! Nay, let us even imagine, as they themselves falsely give out, that some advantage flows from it: it is nothing to the purpose. The question is asked, How are those who have fallen from divine grace restored to it? Scripture everywhere shows the method, but makes no reference to confession, which was long afterwards coined in human brains. What effrontery! to preclude access to the hope of obtaining pardon, unless the confession which they have been pleased to prescribe precedes. The question relates to repentance. Its whole force and nature are so frequently, so copiously, so clearly depicted by the Holy Spirit in the law, the Prophets, and the Gospel, that no doctrine is more lucidly explained. Of confession, such as they pretend, there is throughout a profound silence. Who, then, will believe them 'when they affirm that no repentance is genuine without that appendage, nay, unless it be included in it?

It is enough for me to know the two following things — first, that they devise a Repentance altogether different from that which is recommended to us in Scripture; and secondly, that they enact a condition for obtaining the remission of sins, from which he, to whom alone the power of remitting belongs, wished us to be free. The latter is just as if they were forbidding God to promise salvation without their permission, or at least were opposing his performance of the promise of salvation which he has given. For they do not permit him to pardon our sins, unless it be on the condition of our performing an observance which they alone make binding.

With regard to Satisfaction, they think they make a subtle distinction when they collect the dregs of the vile comments of the sophists, — that not eternal punishment, indeed, but temporal, is to be compensated by satisfaction. Who knew not that such was the prattle of the sophists? And yet, when they pretend that eternal punishment, together with guilt, is remitted to us by confession, or the wish to confess, what else do they mean than that we merit by works what God promises to give freely?

But let us now see the force of the distinction. When the Prophets mention the gratuitous remission of sins, it is true they usually refer to its other effect, viz., that God would be appeased, and no longer avenge the sins of his people or visit them with his rod. Whoever is moderately versed in Scripture will acknowledge the strict accuracy of my statement, that the punishments which we deserved are mitigated, loosed, in fine, abolished, because God pardons us, not for any merit of our own, as if he were appeased by compensation, but because he is moved solely by his own mercy. The Babylonish captivity was a temporal punishment. Its termination in seventy years, when the Israelites deserved it much longer, God ascribes to his own free mercy. Whenever the chastisements which God had threatened are withdrawn, it is uniformly represented as the result of gratuitous reconciliation. It is certainly a relaxation of temporal punishment which God promises in these words, "Not on your account will I do it, but for my name's sake." And Isaiah, when he states, that the satisfaction or price of our peace was laid upon Christ, reminds us that we have not only been freed from punishment by his interposition, but that he bore on our account all the pains by which God is wont to avenge or chastise our sins, in order that we may, however unworthy, enjoy all the blessings of the present life also. (Isaiah 48:9; 53:5.) But God nevertheless still chastises believers. I admit it. But to what end? Is it that he, by inflicting punishment, may pay what is due to himself and his own justice? Not at all; but that he may humble them, by striking them with a dread of his anger, that he may produce in them an earnest feeling of repentance, and render them more cautious in future. But there are means by which they may avert these punishments; I mean, when they anticipate them of their own accord, there is no reason why God should as it were drag them violently. When is there occasion for the rod but just when voluntary correction is wanting? Accordingly, the Apostle tells us that those who shall have judged themselves shall not be judged by the Lord. (1 Corinthians 11:31.)

But how preposterous to infer satisfaction from this? The greater part of believers have, by prayer, warded off the chastisement to which they had made themselves liable. Nay, even Ahab, when he humbles himself spontaneously, feels the hand of God fall lighter upon him. (1 Kings 21:29.) The deprecatory petitions which the saints employed are the most decisive witnesses to gratuitous satisfaction. But these Fathers, it seems, adduce nothing which they cannot prove by passages of Scripture; for Paul teaches, that the sorrow which is agreeable to God worketh: repentance unto salvation not to be repented of. (2 Corinthians 7:10.) What! does Paul here call us back to satisfaction? I hear no word of it. They are dishonestly deluding us. They do so still more in what follows, when they tell us that John must be understood to refer to the same penitence in saying,

"Repent, and bring forth fruits meet for repentance." (Luke 3:8.)

But whom did John address in these terms? Was it not persons who offered themselves for baptism while not yet imbued with the faith of Christ? Somewhat different from this, and yet not less absurd, is their quotation from the second chapter of the Revelations, "Remember whence thou art fallen, and first do works;" whereas the proper reading is, "do the first works," or the former works. The writer exhorts the Ephesians to return to their former state of life. With what face is this stretched to satisfaction? When they so pertly called black white, did they think there would be no eyes to detect their fraud? Lysander once said to deputies who had spoken in a meeting of allies more imperiously than they ought, that they had need of a city which would be very indulgent to them. These masters would need a herd of oxen if they wish to have an audience which they can persuade to believe what they please. Let them go and boast of being guided immediately by the Holy Spirit, while they are palpable falsifiers of holy writ.

To sum up the whole — Though believers ought to be constantly thinking of Repentance, these Holy Fathers imagine it to be an indescribable something of rare occurrence — though Scripture declares repentance to be a renewal of the whole man — though it points out its very source, fear excited by a true sense of the Divine judgment — though it enumerates its parts, self-denial, which consists in a hatred of sin and dissatisfaction with our own depravity, and renewal of life or regeneration of the spirit, which is nothing else than the restoration of the Divine image — though it carefully marks its effects, and explicitly defines its whole nature, — the venerable Fathers produce nothing but the flimsy inanities by which the doctrine of repentance has been corrupted under the Papacy. What was said by ecclesiastical writers concerning external discipline, which referred to the formal profession of repentance, they ignorantly wrest to the spiritual renovation which formed the subject of their discourse. Not to be tedious in reviewing each point, let any one compare their lucubrations with our writings, and he will find and acknowledge that they have turned light into darkness.

I have hitherto endeavored to censure without accusing; and impartial readers will observe, that I censure nothing unless compelled to do so. But there is not a sentence which does not extort more of it from me than I could wish. Of this nature is the assertion under the sixteenth head, that the grace of Justification is lost, not only by unbelief, but by any mortal sin. If they meant that we are ejected from the possession (enjoyment) of this great blessing by an evil conscience, I would not at all gainsay them, I mean as far as regards ourselves. For although God does not cast us off, yet an evil conscience is such a separation from him as excludes us from the enjoyment of a lively and justifying knowledge of his paternal love towards us. But they are preposterous, first, in recognizing no sin as mortal that is not gross and palpable:, whereas most inward sins wound the mind more grievously and even fatally; and, secondly, in not perceiving how a good conscience is the inseparable attendant of faith. Were it not so, how could it be said that our hearts are purified, by faith, that Christ dwells in our hearts by faith, that it is the victory by which we overcome the world, the shield for repelling the assaults of the devil, and that we are kept by faith through the power of God unto salvation? (Acts 15:9; Ephesians 3:17; 1 John 5:4; Ephesians 6:16; 1 Peter 5:9; 1:5.) There is no doubt, therefore, that faith is overwhelmed and buried in a man whenever he has been overcome by any temptation so as to abandon the fear of God. For the Spirit of holiness cannot be separated from faith any more than can Christ himself. I do not assert, however, that when we forsake the fear of the Lord faith is altogether extinguished in us. But as the fear of God is oppressed by depraved lusts, so I say that faith is stifled, and for the time exerts its power no more than if it were in a manner dead. The holy Fathers craftily endeavor to burrow out a hole in which they may hide their impious dogma, that we are not justified by faith alone. Not succeeding in this they attempt another method.

We come now to the last head, which treats of The Merit of Works. Here there is no dispute between us as to the necessity of exhorting 'believers to good works, and even stimulating them by holding forth a reward. What then? First, I differ from them in this, that they make eternal life the reward; for if God rewards works with eternal life, they will immediately make out that faith itself is the reward which is paid, whereas Scripture uniformly proclaims that it is the inheritance which falls to us by no other right than that of free adoption. But there is still greater ground for contradicting, when they are not ashamed to affirm that nothing is to prevent believers from satisfying the Law, at least in a degree proportioned to the present state, and meriting eternal life. Where then will be the blessedness of which David speaks, (Psalm 32,) and without which we are all thrice wretched? Wo to those miserable men who perceive not that he who has come nearest to perfection has not yet advanced half-way! All who have their conscience exercised feel the strict truth of Augustine's sentiment, "The righteousness of saints in this life consists more in the forgiveness of sins than the perfection of virtues." (Lib. de Civit. Dei, 19 c. 27.) Still more accurate is another passage which I quoted, that; "so long as they groan under the infirmity of the flesh, the only hope left them is, that they have a mediator in Christ by whom they are reconciled to God." (Lib. ad Bon., 3. c. 5.)

It is not strange, however, that addle-pated monks who, having never experienced any struggle of conscience, and who, moreover, being intoxicated with ambition, or surfeiting and drunkenness, only desire to raise themselves in the estimation of their idol, should thus prate of the perfection of the Law. With the same confidence do they talk of a heaven for hire, while they themselves meanwhile continue engrossed with the present hire, after which they are always gaping. But in vain do they attempt to dazzle eyes not wholly blind with those fair colors which they

afterwards employ when they prohibit any one from glorying or confid-
ing in works, because they are the gifts of God. Not to mention that what
they now confess to be gifts of God, they previously claimed in a greater
degree for human ability, there are three errors in their decree which are
not to be tolerated. Though they mention incidentally that the good
works of the pious are meritorious by the merit of Christ, they omit the
most necessary part, viz., that there is no work untainted with impurity,
until it be washed away by the blood of Christ. Nay rather, they annex
a false dignity to works, as if they could please without pardon. There
is, indeed, a speciousness in the gloss that they all flow from the Spirit of
Christ. But where will the absolute power of the Holy Spirit be found? Is
it not distributed to every one in measure? (1 Corinthians 12:11.) They
ought, therefore, to have observed, that it is always mixed with dross of
ours which taints its purity. But while our inherent depravity renders
every kind of work which proceeds from us vicious in the sight of God,
the only thing left for our works is to recover the grace which they have
not in themselves, by a gratuitous acceptance. This is done when works
acknowledged to have no value in themselves borrow, and, as it were, beg
their value from Christ.

It is, indeed, a gross and impious delusion, not to acknowledge that
every work which proceeds from us has only one way of obtaining acceptance, viz., when all that was vicious in it is pardoned by paternal in-
dulgence. Another delusion almost similar to this is their not reflecting,
that even if we should have merited anything by any one work, the whole
of the merit, be it what it may, is lost by contrary transgression.

"He who offends in one point is guilty of all." (James 2:10)

What reward do you promise yourself when nothing is produced but
liability to eternal death They are also in error when they do not flee to
the only remedy, and assuming that there is some good thing in them,

ask God of his goodness, to regard it with favor, by not imputing the evil things which far exceed it both in weight and number.

The third error, however, is by far the worst, I mean their making assurance of salvation depend on the view of works. At one time, indeed, they prohibit us from trusting in ourselves, but when they again tell us to look to our works that we may have a sure hope of salvation, what grounds of hope, can we find in them? Do they not plainly place our whole trust in ourselves? Accordingly, they add a clause which is fit only for such a doctrine. It is, that in this life we carry on a warfare of doubtful issue, and cannot attain certainty, until God render to every one according to his works. By this they overthrow all confidence in our faith, or to use Paul's expression, make faith itself void. (Romans 4:14.)

But Paul declares that he is not justified, because he is not conscious of anything in himself. (1 Corinthians 4:4.) This is true, and therefore, in order that our possession of righteousness may be stable and tranquil, our part is to omit all mention of works, and beseech our Judge not to enter into judgment with us. (Psalm 143:2.) We reach the haven of security only when God lays aside the character of Judge, and exhibits himself to us as a Father.

And yet those swinish men are not ashamed to thunder out a cruel denunciation to terrify the simple, that no man is capable of receiving righteousness who does not firmly adhere to whatever they prescribe. What! has a new method of Justification lately appeared? Or rather, as salvation is one, do we not all come to it by one way? What will become of the Prophets and Apostles who gave no heed to such masters? Therefore, paying no regard to the Council of Trent, let us hold that fixed faith which the Prophets and Apostles, by the Spirit of Christ, delivered to us, knowing whence we have learned it. But the venerable Fathers, as if to make it impossible for any man to doubt that they are of the number of those whose mouth, as David exclaims, (Psalm 4:7) is full of cursing and bitterness, proceed, with truculent bluster, to send forth almost as many anathemas as there are individuals among them, and give these the plausible and honorable name of Canons! Yet that I may not seem to act maliciously, as if I had forgotten the moderation I have hitherto observed, I willingly subscribe to the three first. To the rest I will affix brief censures.

ANTIDOTE TO THE CANONS OF THE COUNCIL OF TRENT.

To Canons 1, 2, and 3:, I say, Amen.

CANON 4.

This was answered above, when I explained how Free-will assents to God calling and exciting it. We certainly obey God with our will, but it is with a will which he has formed in us. Those, therefore, who ascribe any proper movement to free-will, apart from the grace of God, do nothing else than rend the Holy Spirit. Paul declares, not that a faculty of willing is given to us, but that the will itself is formed in us, (Philippians 2:13,) so that from none else but God is the assent or obedience of a right will. He acts within, holds our hearts, moves our hearts, and draws us by the inclinations which he has produced in us. So says Augustine. (Lib. de Corrupt. et Grat., c. 14.) What preparation can there be in a heart of iron, 'until by a wondrous change it begins to be a heart of flesh? This, as the Prophet declares, is entirely the work of God. The will of man will, indeed, dissent from God, so long as it continues contrary, but when it has been framed for obedience, the danger of dissenting is removed. But that the efficacy of divine grace is such, that all opposition is beaten down, and we who were unwilling are made obedient, it is not we who assent, but the Lord by the Prophet, when he promises that lie will make us to walk in his precepts; and Christ also, when he says,

"Whosoever hath heard of my Father cometh unto me." (John 6:45.)

CANON 5.

Let us not raise a quarrel about a word. But as by Free-will they understand a faculty of choice perfectly free and unbiassed to either side:, those who affirm that this is merely to use a name without a substance, have the authority of Christ when he says, that they are free whom the Son makes free, and that all others are the slaves of sin. Freedom and slavery are certainly contrary to each other. As to the term itself, let them hear Augustine, who maintains that the human will is not free so long as it is subject to passions which vanquish and enthral it. (Epist. 144, ad Anastas.) Elsewhere he says, "The will being vanquished by the depravity into which it has fallen, nature is without freedom." (Hom. 3, in Joann.) Again, "Man making a bad use of free-will lost both himself and it." Again, "Man received great powers of free-will when he was created, but lost them by sinning. Foolish men consider not that in the term freewill freedom is implied. But if they are the slaves of sin, why do they boast of free-will? For of whom a man is overcome, to the same is he bound a slave." Nay, in another place he openly derides the name. "The will," says he, "is free, not freed — free to righteousness, the slave of sin! Why, then, do they so much inflame miserable men by reminding them of their slavery, but just that they might learn to flee to the deliverer?" (Aug. de Perfect. Justit. Lib. de Verb. Apost. Serm. 3; De Spiritu et Litera, c. 30; De Corrupt. et Grat., c. 13.)

CANON 6.

As I abhor paradox, I readily repudiate the saying that the treachery of Judas is as properly the work of God as the calling of Paul. But they never will convince any man that God only acts permissively in the wicked, except it be one who is ignorant of the whole doctrine of Scripture. When it is said that the reprobate are set apart to execute the work of God; that his are the snares, swords, and axes which are directed by his hand; that his hiss arouses them to execute what his hand and counsel have decreed; that Christ was slain 'by the Jews by the determinate counsel of God, (Isaiah 10:5; Ezekiel 17:20; 32:2; Psalm 17:13; Acts 2:4, 23) the words are too strong to be evaded by the subterfuge of permission. Augustine interprets better. After quoting the passages of Scripture in which the Father is said to have delivered up the Son, and Christ to have delivered himself, he immediately adds, "What, then, did Judas do but sin?" Nor can he be justly blamed for saying elsewhere, that "God worketh in the hearts of men to incline their wills as he pleaseth, whether to good, of his mercy, or to evil, according to their deservings, and that by his judgment, sometimes open, sometimes hidden, but always just;" for he immediately adds the qualification, that "the malice is not his." (De Verb. Dom. Serm. 63.) In like manner he had said a little before, "He does not command the wicked by ordering, in which case obedience would be laudable, but by his secret and just judgment he bends their will, already bad by their own depravity, to this misdeed or that." (Aug. de Gr. et Lib. Arb. c. 21.) For there is nothing here but what the Scriptures teach almost in the same words when they speak of inclining and turning, hardening and doing.

CANON 7.

Assuredly a bad tree can only produce bad fruit. But who will be so shameless as to deny that we are bad trees until we are ingrafted into Christ? Therefore, if any good fruit is praised in man, let the root of it be sought in faith, as Augustine admonishes, (in Psalm 31 Sermon 1.) There God so often declares that he regards not the outward appearance, but looketh on the heart. This is said expressly by Jeremiah. (Jeremiah 5.) But what can be the cleanness or sincerity of a heart which Peter tells us is purified only by faith? (Acts 15:9.) Admirably, therefore, does Augustine say to Boniface, "Our religion distinguishes the just from the unjust, not by the law of works, but by the law of faith, without which the works which seem good turn to sin." He adds, "Therefore unbelievers sin in whatever they do, because they do not refer their doings to a lawful end." (Lit. ad Bonif., Lib. 3, c. 5.) He treats copiously of the same subject in his tract against Julian. Hence, also, in another place he describes theirs as a wandering course, inasmuch as the more active they are, the farther they are carried from the goal, and. the more therefore their condition becomes hopeless. At last he concludes, that "it is better to limp in the course than keep running out of it." (Praef. in Psalm 31.) And what more would we, have? Let them anathematize the Apostle, who declares that without faith it is impossible to please God! (Hebrews 11:6.) Let them anathematize Christ and Paul, who declare that all unbelievers are dead, and are raised from death by the gospel! (John 5; Ephesians 2:1.)

CANON 8.

I answer: AMEN. Nor do I think that the thing ever came into any man's mind. For being such as is described by them, it comprehends true repentance and is conjoined with faith. On the subject of the servile fear of hell, which to some degree restrains unbelievers from rushing with such furious and headlong impetus into wicked courses, we are of the same sentiments as Augustine, whose words are, (Ad. Anast. Ep. 144,) "What man is found innocent before God, who, if fear were withdrawn, would do what God forbids? He is guilty in his will by wishing to do what cannot lawfully be done. As far as he is concerned, he would rather that there was no justice prohibiting and punishing sin. And hence, if he would rather that there was no justice, who can doubt that he would take it away if he could? How then is he righteous who is such an enemy to righteousness, that if power were given him he would take it away when commanding, and not bear it when threatening or judging? He, therefore, is the enemy of righteousness who does not sin, because he is afraid of punishment. And, indeed, when all the progress made is that the sinner curbed by terror murmurs against God, who can deny that by such contumacy he aggravates his sin?"

CANON 9.

This Canon is very far from being canonical; for it joins things which are utterly at variance. They imagine that a man is justified by faith without any movement of his own will, as if it were not with the heart that a man believeth unto righteousness. Between them and us there is this difference, that they persuade themselves that the movement comes from the man himself, whereas we maintain that faith is voluntary, because God draws our wills to himself. Add, that when we say a man is justified by faith alone, we do not fancy a faith devoid of charity, but we mean that faith alone is the cause of justification.

CANON 10.

Could these anathemas take effect, all who are not versed in the sophistical art would pay dearly for their simplicity. They formerly asserted in their decrees that the righteousness of God was the only formal cause of Justification; now they anathematize those who say that we are formally righteous by the obedience of Christ. But it is in another sense. I see it or scent it. But how few are there who will not be misled by the ambiguity? Although it may be that having met with the sentiment somewhere and not understood it, they boldly condemn it. For as it were impious to say that the righteousness of Christ is only an exemplar or type to us, so if any one were to teach that we are righteous formally, i.e., not by quality but by imputation, meaning that our righteousness is in relation merely, there would be nothing worthy of censure. The adverb formally is used in both senses.

CANON 11.

I wish the reader to understand that as often as we mention Faith alone in this question, we are not thinking of a dead faith, which worketh not by love, but holding faith to be the only cause of justification. (Galatians 5:6; Romans 3:22.) It is therefore faith alone which justifies, and yet the faith which justifies is not alone: just as it is the heat alone of the sun which warms the earth, and yet in the sun it is not alone, because it is constantly conjoined with light. Wherefore we do not separate the whole grace of regeneration from faith, but claim the power and faculty of justifying entirely for faith, as we ought. And yet it is not us that these Tridentine Fathers anathematize so much as Paul, to whom we owe the definition that the righteousness of man consists in the forgiveness of sins. The words are in the fourth chapter to the Romans,

"David speaketh of the blessedness of the man to whom God imputeth righteousness without works, saying, Blessed are those whose iniquities are forgiven." (Psalm 32:1)

We see that in Paul's view blessedness and righteousness mean the same thing. And where does he place both but solely in the remission of sins? His meaning is the same as in the fifth chapter of the Second Epistle to the Corinthians, "God was in Christ reconciling the world unto himself, not imputing unto men their trespasses." For he immediately explains how that reconciliation comes to us: "We are ambassadors beseeching you as in the name of Christ. He made him who knew no sin to be sin for us, that we might be the righteousness of God in him." See how being reconciled to God by the sacrifice of Christ, we both are accounted and are righteous in him. But why quote one passage after another, while this is the doctrine uniformly inculcated by Prophets and Apostles?

It is worth while to observe how dexterously they accommodate Scripture to their purpose. They say that the love which is shed abroad in our hearts by the Holy Spirit must not be excluded. Thus they corrupt one passage by another. The context shows that Paul does not there speak of our own love, but of the paternal love of God toward us; for he holds it forth as ground of consolation in all circumstances of adversity, that the Spirit suggests proof of the divine benevolence towards us. This swinish herd, on the contrary, twist it to mean, that we are not ashamed of hoping because we love God. And the moment they have given utterance to the words they insist on being regarded as oracles! With similar perversion they make justifying grace a habit, and deny that it proceeds from the free favor of God. The words of Scripture are clear as day against them. For when Paul says, that to believers reward is imputed not as of debt but of grace; and again, that the inheritance is of faith that it may be of grace, (Romans 4:4,) how is it possible in expounding it to give it any other meaning than that of free favor? What else is meant by a purpose of grace? One of the most striking passages is the first chapter to the Ephesians, where, going on word by word, he tells us that the Father hath made us acceptable to himself in the Son.

CANON 12.

The venerable Fathers will not allow Justifying Faith to be defined as the confidence with which we embrace the mercy of God as forgiving sin for Christ's sake. But it pleases the Holy Spirit, who thus speaks by the mouth of Paul,

"We are justified freely by the grace of God, through the redemption which is in Christ, whom God hath appointed a propitiation through faith in his blood for the remission of sins which are past." (Romans 3:24.)

Nor is it possible to give a different exposition to what he afterwards says, viz., that

"being justified by faith we have peace with God." (Romans 5:1.)

How so, but just that our consciences are never at ease until they rest in the mercy of God? This he distinctly expresses immediately after, when he adds the reason, that the love of God is shed abroad in our hearts by the Holy Spirit, as being the witness of our free adoption, and not the witness only, but also the earnest and seal. Again, "We have boldness and access with confidence through faith in him." For the same reason he calls the gospel, rather than the law, "the doctrine of faith." He moreover declares, that the gospel is "the message of reconciliation."

CANON 13.

That, however, is Paul's meaning when he concludes, that if Faith is made void the promise is abolished. (Romans 4:14.) That too is the meaning of the term plhroforia which Paul also sometimes uses. Accordingly he regards the eyes of our mind as not duly enlightened unless we perceive what is the hope of our inheritance. It is also sufficiently obvious from the above passages, that faith is not right unless we dare with tranquil minds to sist ourselves into the divine presence. For, as Bernard admirably expresses it, (Super Cantic. Sermon 16 c. 3, 10,) "If conscience is troubled, it will not be troubled out of measure, because it will remember the words of our Lord. Therein the infirm have firm rest and security." To the same effect are the words of Zechariah, "Each one will come to his own vine, and dwell safely under his own fig-tree, when the iniquity of the land shall have been forgiven."

CANON 14.

I see not why they should condemn the same thing twice, unless it be they were afraid that their first thunderbolt had fallen scatheless! But, though they should fulminate a hundred times they will not be able to prevail in the least degree against this clear truth of God. Christ says, "Son, be of good cheer, thy sins are forgiven thee." This sentence the horned Fathers abominate, whenever any one teaches that acquittal is completed by faith alone. And yet the pious reader ought to remember that we do not exclude repentance, which is altogether necessary, but mention faith only when the inquiry relates to the cause of acquittal. And justly do we so. For how can any one begin truly to fear God unless he is persuaded that God is propitious to him? And whence this persuasion but from confidence in acquittal?

CANON 15.

It is indeed true that to pry too minutely into this matter is hurtful, and therefore to be avoided; but that knowledge of Predestination which Paul recommends dreads neither the stern trident of Neptune, nor all the blasts of Aeolus, nor the thunders of the Cyclops, nor any violence of tempests. For he wishes the Ephesians to know and be assured that they have been made partakers of heavenly grace in Christ, as they had been chosen in him before the foundation of the world. (Ephesians 1:4.) Thus therefore it becomes all believers to be assured of their election, that they may learn to behold it in Christ as in a mirror. Nor is it to no purpose that Christ animates his followers by this consoling reflection — that not one of those whom the Father hath given him shall perish. (John 6:39.) What else, good Sirs, is a certain knowledge of our Predestination than that testimony of adoption which Scripture makes common to all the godly?

CANON 16.

That I may not be forced often to repeat the same thing, what they here condemn is nothing else than what I have previously shown to have been delivered by the same oracles of the Holy Spirit.

CANON 17.

The words of Luke are,

"All who had been pre-ordained to life believed." (Acts 13:48.)

He intimates whence it was that in one audience such a difference existed that some believed, and others persisted in their obstinacy. In like manner Paul asserts, that those are called whom God has previously chosen. (Romans 8:29.) Are not also the reprobate called? Not effectually. For there is this difference in the calling of God, that he invites all indiscriminately by his word, whereas he inwardly calls the elect alone, as Christ says,

"All that the Father hath given me will come to me." (John 6:37.)

In short, if any man is ignorant that the Spirit of regeneration is given to none but the regenerate, I know not what part of Scripture he holds.

CANON 18.

Were Regeneration perfected in this life the observance of the law would be possible. But seeing that believers as long as they live here only perceive the goal at a distance, and with much difficulty keep panting towards it, where is the perfection of obedience, of which those men dream, to be found? But there is no wonder that they prate so boldly of things they know not. War is pleasant to those who never tried it.

CANON 19.

AMEN.

CANON 20.

While no sane man will strike off the yoke of God from the shoulders of believers, as if they behooved not to keep his Commandments, it must still be understood that assurance of salvation by no means depends on the observance of them. For the words of Paul always hold true, that the difference between the Law and the Gospel lies in this, that the latter does not like the former promise life under the condition of works, but from faith. What can be clearer than the antithesis — "The righteousness of the law is in this wise, The man who doeth these things shall live in them.

But the righteousness which is of faith speaketh thus, Whoso believeth," etc. (Romans 10:5.) To the same effect is this other passage,

"If the inheritance were of the law, faith would be made void and the promise abolished. Therefore it is of faith that in respect of grace the promise might be sure to every one that believeth." (Romans 4:14.)

As to ecclesiastical laws, they must themselves see to them: we acknowledge one Legislator, to whom it belongs to deliver the rule of life, as from him we have life.

CANON 21.

No one says so. The Fathers, therefore, are anathematizing their own figments, unless perhaps they are offended because we deny that Christ as a lawgiver delivered new laws to the world. That he did so they imagined foolishly. Neither did Moses testify in vain that the Law which he had brought was the way of life and death, (Deuteronomy 30:19;) and again, "This is the way, walk ye in it;" nor in vain do the Prophets and Apostles, whenever they discourse of the true and entire perfection of righteousness, call us back to the law; nor in vain did Christ reply to the Pharisee,

"If thou wouldst enter into life, keep the commandments." (Matthew 19:17; Luke 18:20.)

Accordingly, when Paul charges the law with weakness, he does not place the defect in its teaching, as if it could not bestow life but in our flesh. (Romans 7:8.)

CANON 22.

AMEN.

CANON 23.

We condemn those who affirm that a man once justified cannot sin, and likewise those who deny that the truly justified ever fall: those in like manner who assert that a man regenerated by the Spirit of God is able to abstain even from the least sins. These are the delirious dreams of fanatics, who either with devilish arrogance deceive, or with hypocrisy fascinate the minds of men, or plot to lead them to the precipice of despair. As to the special privilege of the Virgin Mary, when they produce the celestial diploma we shall believe what they say: for to what do they here give the name of the Church, but just to the Council of Clermont? Augustine was certainly a member of the Church, and though he in one passage chooses, in order to avoid obloquy, rather to be silent respecting the blessed Virgin, he uniformly, without making her an exception, describes the Whole race of Adam as involved in sin. Nay, he even almost in distinct terms classes her among sinners, when writing to Marcellinus, he says, They err greatly who hold that any of the saints except Christ require not to use this prayer, "Forgive us our debts." In so doing, they by no means please the saints whom they laud. Chrysostom and Ambrose, who suspect her of having been tempted by ambition, were members of the Church. All these things I mention for no other end but to let my readers understand that there is no figment so nugatory as not to be classed by these blockheads among the Articles of Faith.

CANON 24.

That God visits the good works of the godly with reward, and to former adds new and ampler grace, we deny not. But whosoever asserts that works have the effect of increasing justification, understands neither what is the meaning of justification nor its cause. That we are regarded as righteous when we are accepted by God, has already been proved. From this acceptance, too, works derive whatever grace they had.

CANON 25.

Solomon is correct when he says that

"the ways of a man seem right in his own eyes, but God weigheth the heart." (Proverbs 16:2.)

For how comes it that the horned men of Trent pour forth this execration, but just because they try things by the false balance of their own
opinion, not by the weights of God? In the judgment of God nothing is
genuine and good, save what flows from perfect love to Him. If the heart
of man is never reformed so far in this life, as not to labor under many
defects, and to be distracted by various passions, and often fielded by
worldly allurements, works must of necessity carry some taint along with
them. There is no work, therefore, which is not sin, unless it acquires a
value in consequence of a gratuitous estimate.

CANON 26.

Such boldness is not strange in men who have never felt any serious
fear of the Divine judgment. Let them, if they will, expect eternal life for
their good works; only let us on the authority of Paul hope for it from
the grace of God. But it may be said that in thus speaking of grace they
do not overthrow it. Although they leave the name of grace to a certain
extent, yet so long as consciences in seeking out the cause of salvation
look around for works, wo to them! If they waver with trepidation,
they have fallen from the certainty of faith: and wo again if they dare
to promise themselves any certainty, for they are inflated with devilish
presumption! Let the saying of Paul then stand fast — that

"the inheritance is not of the law but of faith, that the promise according to grace may be sure to every one that believeth." (Romans 4:14.)

CANON 27.

As we acknowledge and feel that every sin, inasmuch as it is condemned by the law of God, is mortal, so the Holy Spirit teaches that
all sins flow from unbelief, or, at least, from deficiency of faith. Eternal death is indeed the curse which God denounces against adulterers,
thieves, and false witnesses; but wherever faith reigns it expels all sin, and

so averts the Divine anger in the same way in which one extinguishes a fire by withdrawing the fuel.

CANON 28.

I deny not that, even during the most grievous lapses, some seed of Faith remains, though in a smothered state. However small it is, I admit that it partakes of the nature of true faith: I add, living faith, since otherwise no fruit could come from it. But since it does not appear for a time, nor exhibit itself by the usual signs, it is, in respect of our sense, as if it were dead. But nothing of this kind entered the minds of the Fathers or their dictatorial monks. All they wished was to establish their absurd dogma of an informal and a formal faith. Hence they maintain that faith to be true which is manifestly dead; as if faith could be the life of the soul, (as Augustine, in accordance with the uniform doctrine of Scripture, elegantly terms it,)and yet not be itself alive. To the same purpose they contend that men are Christians though they have no charity, and anathematize those who think otherwise; in other words, according to them, we anathematize the Holy Spirit if we deride a false profession of Christianity, and set it at naught. Paul pronounced them no Israelites who were not truly the children of Abraham. He moreover defines true Christianity as consisting in "the putting off of the old man;" and he declares that God is denied by those "who do not live godly."

CANON 29.

The first article, along with its author, Novatus, we also execrate. As to the second, if the lapsed can only be reinstated in grace by the Sacrament of Penance, what will become of Peter, who, after his dreadful fall, had no access to the remedy which they require as of absolute necessity? Nay, what will become of the tens of thousands in those ages which know nothing of that Auricular Confession which they now represent as the gate of salvation? As to their glorying in the teaching of Christ and his

Apostles, their effrontery is extreme, seeing it is clear, from their own historians, that for four hundred years there was no law on the subject of Confession. Therefore, if they would obtain credit for their wicked figments, it will be necessary for them not only to exterminate all the monuments of antiquity, but also to deprive mankind of all sense and judgment!

CANON 30.

They think that, after the guilt is remitted, the liability. to punishment remains, But Scripture everywhere describes, as the fruit of forgiven guilt, that God withdraws his chastisements, and, forgetting his wrath and revenge, blesses us. And when David proclaims those blessed "to whom the Lord imputeth not sin," he not only refers to the remission of guilt, but speaks chiefly of punishment. And what, pray, will be the end or limit, should God begin to exact punishment for sins which are both in number infinite and in weight so heavy, that the hundredth part would sink us to the lowest hell? It is easy indeed for Fathers intoxicated with devilish presumption to call for temporal punishment. To them scarcely anything short of murder is a sin; whoredom is a trivial mistake — the foulest lusts praiseworthy trials of virtue, a hidden wound of the conscience, a mere bagatelle. But to us, who, after long examination, feeling as it were confused and overwhelmed, are forced at length to break out into these words with David, "Who can understand his errors?" the mode of escape is not so easy. Still we deny not, that sometimes after the guilt is forgiven, God chastises us, but it is in the way of admonition and correction — not vengeance. Their idea that punishment is exacted by the justice of God is therefore a profane fiction. All are not punished in the same way, nor in proportion to their faults; but just according as God knows the application of the rod to be necessary, in order that each, under the training of discipline, may act more wisely in future.

The Fathers, however, here demonstrate what industrious architects they are. Out of one little word they construct a labyrinth composed of a thousand labyrinths. The abyss which they say swallowed up all souls must surely be of immense extent. We see indeed that all the riches of the world are engulfed in it! They ought at least to have spent a little more labor in the construction. There is no mention of Purgatory at all in any part of Scripture. But, as Augustine says, (Ep. 157, ad Optat.,) when a matter naturally obscure cannot be comprehended by us, and Scripture does not come distinctly to our aid, human conjecture is presumptuous in giving any decision. What then must our conclusion be, but that these men act presumptuously in daring, out of their own brains, to make a fabric of that which has no foundation in the word of God? unless, perhaps, they would have us to receive their device of Purgatory as a kind of vaticination vented by ventriloquism; for there is nothing which serves so well to fill their bellies! But what of this? Purgatory cannot stand without destroying the whole truth of Scripture. The demonstration of this would be long, but it is clearly given in our writings. In short, when satisfactions are overthrown, Purgatory of necessity tumbles along with them.

CANON 31.

I acknowledge that he who is truly justified will not forget that a reward is laid up for him, but be incited by it as the best stimulus to well-doing. And yet he will not look to this alone; for seeing that God requires an ingenuous obedience from his children, he will not only repudiate slavish observance of this description, but utterly reject it. Accordingly, the Holy Spirit, in every part of Scripture, as well as in those words which he puts into the mouth of Paul in the first chapter of the Ephesians, assigns a very different motive to a pious and holy life.

CANON 32.

By what right or in what sense the Good Works which the Spirit of Christ performs in us are called ours, Augustine briefly teaches when the draws an analogy from the Lord's Prayer: saying, that the bread which we there ask is called "ours" on no other ground than simply that it is given to us. Accordingly, as the same writer elsewhere teaches, no man will embrace the gifts of Christ till he has forgotten his own merits. He sometimes gives the reason: because, what is called merit is naught else but the free gift of God. Let us therefore allow these Fathers to bawl out, that by separating merit from grace:, we are wickedly lacerating what is truly one. He who has learned from our former observations wherein it is that the merit of works consists, will not be greatly dismayed art the sound of the present anathema.

CANON 33.

A very ingenious caution! no man is to see what every man sees! They almost go the length of making void both the glory of God and the grace of Christ. Meanwhile they hurl a dire execration at any one who presumes to think that they derogate in any respect from either. It is just as if a man were to murder another in the open market-place before the eyes of the public, and yet prohibit any one from believing that the murder thus manifest to all has been really committed. Moreover, the rats here turn informers against themselves, by holding out an anathema in terrorem against all who shall dare to perceive the impiety of which they themselves are conscious.

SEVENTH SESSION OF THE COUNCIL OF TRENT.

F or the completion of the salutary doctrine concerning Justification which was promulgated with the unanimous consent of all the Fathers in the foregoing last Session, it has seemed suitable to treat of the most Holy Sacraments of The Church, by which all true righteousness either begins, or when begun is increased, or when lost is repaired. Wherefore, The Holy, (Ecumenical, and General Council of Trent, lawfully met in the Holy Spirit, under the presidency of the foresaid Legates of the Holy See, in order to banish errors, and extirpate the heresies which in this our time have both been stirred up from heresies of old condemned by our Fathers, and invented anew in regard to the most holy sacraments, and which greatly obstruct the purity of the Catholic Church, and the salvation of souls, has deemed it proper, in adhering to the doctrine of the Holy Scriptures, the Apostolical Traditions, and the

Consent of the Councils and Fathers, to enact and decree these present Canons, intending afterwards, with the help of the Divine Spirit, to publish the others which are required to complete the work thus begun.

OF THE SACRAMENTS IN GENERAL.

I. Whosoever shall say that the Sacraments of the New Law were not all instituted by our Lord Jesus Christ, and are either more or fewer than seven, viz., Baptism, Confirmation, the Eucharist, Penance, Extreme Unction, Orders, and Matrimony, or even that any one of these seven is not truly and properly a Sacrament, let him be anathema.

II. Whosoever shall say that these said Sacraments of the New Law differ not from the Sacraments of the Old Law, except that the ceremonies are different, and the external rites different, let him be anathema.

III. Whosoever shall say that these seven Sacraments are so equal among themselves, that no one is in any respect of greater dignity than another, let him be anathema.

IV. Whosoever shall say that the Sacraments of the New Law are not necessary to salvation, but superfluous, and that without them or a with for them, men by faith alone obtain the grace of justification, though all are not necessary for each, let him be anathema.

V. Whosoever shall say that these Sacraments were instituted for the sake of nourishing faith alone, let him be anathema.

VI. Whosoever shall say that the Sacraments of the New Law do not contain the grace which they signify, or do not confer grace itself on those placing no obstacle to it, as if they were only external signs of a grace or righteousness received by faith, and a kind of badges of Christian profession, by which believers are distinguished among men from unbelievers, let him be anathema.

VII. Whosoever shall say that grace is not given by Sacraments of this kind, always and to all, as far as depends on the part of God, although they are duly received, but sometimes, and to some persons, let him be anathema.

VIII. Whosoever shall say that by these Sacraments of the New Law grace is not conferred, *ex opere operato*, (from the work performed,) but that faith alone in the Divine promise suffices to obtain grace, let him be anathema.

IX. Whosoever shall say that in the three Sacraments, namely, Baptism, Confirmation, and Orders, there is not impressed on the soul a character, i.e., some spiritual and indelible sign, owing to which they cannot be repeated, let him be anathema.

X. Whosoever shall say that all Christians have right to administer the word and all the Sacraments, let him be anathema.

XI. Whosoever shall say that in ministers, when they perform and distribute the Sacraments, an intention, at least, of doing what the Church does, is not requisite, let him be anathema.

XII. Whosoever shall say that a minister, in a state of mortal sin, provided he has observed all the essentials which pertain to the performing and giving of a Sacrament, does not perform or give the Sacrament, let him be anathema.

XIII. Whosoever shall say that the received and approved Rites of the Catholic Church, accustomed to be used in the solemn administration of the Sacraments, may either be despised or omitted, at pleasure, by the minister, without sin, or changed into other new rites, by any pastors of churches, let him be anathema.

OF BAPTISM.

I. Whosoever shall say that the Baptism of John had the same three as the Baptism of Christ, let him be anathema.

II. Whosoever shall say that true and natural water is not of necessity in baptism, and shall accordingly give some metaphorical twist to those words of our Lord Jesus Christ, — "Unless a man be born of water and of the Spirit," let him be anathema.

III. Whosoever shall say that in the Roman Church (which is the mother and mistress of all Churches) there is not the true doctrine of the Sacrament of Baptism, let him be anathema.

IV. Whosoever shall say that the baptism, which is also given by heretics in the name of the Father, and of the Son, and of the Holy Spirit, with the intention of doing what the Church does, is not true baptism, let him be anathema.

V. Whosoever shall say that baptism is free, i.e., not necessary to salvation, let him be anathema.

VI. Whosoever shall say that a baptized person cannot lose grace, even though he will it, how much soever he may sin, if he be not unwilling to believe, let him be anathema.

VII. Whosoever shall say that the baptized become by baptism itself only debtors to faith alone, but not to observe the whole Law of Christ, let him be anathema.

VIII. Whosoever shall say that the baptized are free from all the precepts of the Holy Church, which have been either written or handed down, so that they are not bound to observe them, unless they are willing to submit to them of their own accord, let him be anathema.

IX. Whosoever shall say that men are to be recalled to the remembrance of the baptism they received, so that they may understand that all the vows which are made after baptism are void, by virtue of the promise made in said baptism, as if those vows detracted from the faith which they professed, and from baptism itself, let him be anathema.

X. Whosoever shall say that all the sins which are done after baptism are either discharged or made venial by the mere remembrance and faith of baptism received, let him be anathema.

XI. Whosoever shall say that true and duly conferred baptism is to be repeated to him who has denied the faith of Christ among infidels, after he turns to repentance, let him be anathema.

XII. Whosoever shall say that no man is to be baptized, unless at that age at which Christ was baptized, or at the very point of death, let him be anathema.

XIII. Whosoever shall say that infants, in respect they have no act (capacity) of believing, are not to be counted among believers after they have received baptism, and therefore are to be re-baptized after they come to the years of discretion, or that it is better that the baptism of them be omitted, than that they, not believing by their own act, be baptized in the faith only of the Church, let him be anathema.

XIV. Whosoever shall say that such infants, when they grow up, are to be interrogated whether they are willing to ratify what their godfathers promised in their name when they Were baptized; and when they answer that they are not willing, are to be left to their own will and not forced to a Christian life in the meanwhile by some punishment, except that they are to be kept back from receiving the Eucharist, and other Sacraments, until they repent, let him be anathema.

OF CONFIRMATION.

I. Whosoever shall say that the Confirmation of Baptism is an idle ceremony, and not rather a true and proper Sacrament, or that anciently it was nothing else than a kind of catechizing, by which those on the eve of adolescence explained the reason of their faith in presence of the Church, let him be anathema.

II. Whosoever shall say that those who attribute any virtue to chrism in the Sacrament of Confirmation insult the Holy Spirit, let him be anathema.

III. Whosoever shall say that the ordinary minister of holy Confirmation is not the bishop alone, but any simple priest, let him be anathema.

DECREES ON REFORMATION.

The same Holy Council, the same Legates presiding, intending to prosecute the business of Residence and Reformation already commenced, unto the praise of God and increase of the Christian Religion, have thought proper to enact as follows, always without prejudice to the authority of the Apostolic See.

For the government of Cathedral Churches, let no one, unless born of lawful wedlock, and of mature age, gravity of manners, and skill in literature, according to the constitution of Alexander III., which begins, "Whereas in all," promulgated in the Lateran Council, be held qualified.

Let no man, however conspicuous in dignity, rank, or preeminence, presume either to accept or hold at the same time more than one Metropolitan or Cathedral Church by title or *in Commendam*, or under any other name, contrary to the ordinances of the Sacred Canons, since he is to be regarded as very happy to whose lot it; has fallen to govern one Church well and fruitfully, and with safety to the souls committed to him. Let those who now hold several Churches, contrary to the tenor of the present decree, after choosing the one which they wish to retain, be bound to demit the others within six months, if they are at the free disposal of the Apostolic See, or, if otherwise, within a year. Otherwise let the Churches themselves, the last obtained only excepted, be considered *ipso facto* vacant.

Let inferior Ecclesiastical Benefices, especially those having a cure of souls, be conferred on fit and worthy persons, who may be able to reside on the spot, and discharge the cure in person, according to the constitution of Alexander III in the Lateran Council, beginning, "As some," and another of Gregory, published in the General Council of Lyons, beginning, "Although the Canon." Let any collation or provision made otherwise be held null and void, and let the ordinary giving' collation know that he will incur the penalties of the consti,mtion of the General Council, beginning, "Too heavy."

Whosoever, in future, shall have presumed to accept and hold at the same time several Cures, or otherwise incompatible Ecclesiastical Benefices, whether by way of union for life, or of perpetual *Commendam*, or under any other name and title whatsoever, against the form of the Sacred Canons, and especially the constitution of Innocent III., which begins, "Of much," let him be deprived of the benefices, according to the appointment of said constitution *ipso jure*, and also in virtue of the present Canon.

Let the Ordinaries of the places compel all persons whatsoever holding several Cures, or otherwise incompatible Ecclesiastical Benefices, to exhibit their dispensations, and in other respects let them proceed according to the constitution of Gregory X., published in the General Council of Lyons, beginning, "The Ordinaries," which constitution this Holy Council thinks ought to be renewed, and renews it; adding, moreover, that the Ordinaries themselves, even by the deputation of fit vicars, and the assignation of a suitable portion of the fruits, must by all means take care that the cure of souls be in no respect neglected, and the benefices themselves least of all defrauded of due services, — appeals, privileges, and exemptions of whatever sort, even with the deputation of special judges, and interdicts by them being available to none in the matters aforesaid.

Perpetual Unions within the last forty years may be examined by the Ordinaries as delegates of the Apostolic See, and those which have been obtained by subreption or obreption be declared void. Let those which were granted within the time aforesaid, but have not yet obtained effect, in whole or in part, and those which shall hereafter be made at the instance of any individual, unless it shall appear that they were made from lawful. Or otherwise reasonable causes, to be verified before the Ordinary of the place, those interested being called, be presumed to have been obtained surreptitiously; and, therefore, let them be altogether without force, unless it shall have been otherwise declared by the Apostolic See.

Let Ecclesiastical Benefices with cure, which are found perpetually united and annexed to Cathedral, Collegiate, or other Churches, and also Monasteries, Benefices, or Colleges, or pious places whatsoever, be visited every year by the Ordinaries of the places, who must be solicitously careful to provide that the cure of souls be laudably performed by fit perpetual vicars, (unless a different arrangement should seem to said Ordinaries to be expedient for the good government of the churches,) to be appointed to the same by them, with a portion (greater or less, at the discretion of said Ordinaries) of the thirds of the fruits to be allocated over a certain subject, — appeals, privileges, exemptions, even with the deputations of judges, and any interdicts of theirs whatsoever being of no force in the matters aforesaid.

Let the Ordinaries of the places be bound to visit all Churches whatsoever, however exempted, once a year with Apostolical authority; and provide, by suitable remedies of *law*, that those things which need reparation be repaired, and the churches be by no means defrauded of the cure of souls (if any belongs to them) and other due services; appeals, privileges, customs, even those having the prescription of time immemorial, the deputations of judges and their interdicts being utterly excluded.

Let those promoted to greater Churches receive the rite of conse-cration within the time appointed by law, and let prorogations granted beyond six months be available to none.

When a See is vacant, it may not be lawful for the Chapter, within a year from the date of the vacancy, to grant license of ordaining, or letters dimissory or reverend, (as some call them,) as well according to the arrangement of the common law, as also in virtue of any privilege or custom whatsoever, to any one who is not constrained by the occasion of an ecclesiastical benefice received or to be received. If it be done oth-erwise, let the Chapter contravening be liable to ecclesiastical interdict; and those thus ordained, if in inferior orders, enjoy no clerical privilege, especially in criminal matters, and if in higher orders, be suspended, *ipso jure*, from exercising the order, at the pleasure of the future prelate.

Let faculties *de paromovendo* not be obtained by any one whatsoever, unless those having a lawful cause why they cannot be ordained by their own bishops, to be expressed in the letters; and even then let them not be ordained, except by a bishop residing in his diocese, or by one exer-cising the pontifical functions in his stead; and after a careful previous examination.

Let faculties *de non promovendo*, except those granted in cases provid-ed for by law, be effectual only for a year.

Let none presented or elected, or named by any ecclesiastical persons whatsoever, even by the Nuncios of the Apostolic See, be instituted, confirmed, or admitted to any Ecclesiastical Benefices, even under the pretext of any privilege or custom prescribed by time immemorial, unless they have been previously examined and found fit by the Ordinaries of the place; and let them not be able, by means of any appeal, to screen themselves from the obligation to undergo trial, — those presented, chosen, or named by Universities or Colleges of general literature excepted.

In cases of exemption, let the constitution of Innocent IV., beginning "Wishing," published in the General Council of Lyons, be observed, which constitution the present Holy Council has judged proper to renew, and renews: Adding, moreover, in the case of civil causes for wages, and those of indigent persons, secular clergy, or regulars not living in monasteries, however exempted, although they should have on the spot a certain judge deputed by the Apostolic See; and in these causes, if they have no such judge, let them be convened before the Ordinaries of the bounds as delegated to this effect by said See, and be forced and compelled, by legal means, to pay the debt, — no privileges, exemptions, deputations of conservators and their interdicts being of any avail against the aforesaid.

Let Ordinaries take care that all Hospitals be faithfully and carefully managed by their administrators, under whatever named called, or however exempted; observing the form of the constitution of the Council of Vienna, beginning "As it happens:" which constitution the Holy Council has deemed proper to renew, and renews, with the exceptions therein contained

ANTIDOTE TO THE SEVENTH SESSION

How much sweat must be spent in any contest where a bad cause is pleaded, the venerable Fathers had experienced in last Session. Therefore, that they might not over-fatigue themselves by a second conflict, they preferred to return to their compendious method of settling the matter by fulmination. And, indeed, it was unbecoming their dictatorial style to undergo the trouble of rendering a reason. What then! The Corybantes sound their brass and redouble the clang. Tremble, boys! Whoever possesses a spark of manly courage will despise their futile crepitations, and boldly, with unruffled mind, inquire into the contents of their decrees. How they teem with stupid absurdities I engage to demonstrate with my finger.

CANON 1.

They insist that Seven Sacraments were instituted by Christ. Why, then, did they not order him to institute them? The number Seven which they place under the sanction of an anathema has not only no support from Scripture, but none even from any approved author. This is little. Of the Sacraments which they enumerate we show that some were temporary, as the anointing of the sick, and others, falsely so called, as matrimony. The arguments by which we evince this are plain and strong. What! will they boast that they have the gift of healing? If anointing is the symbol of that gift, are they not apes when they use it without the reality? Again, what promise is there in this ceremony that have any application to us? If a sacrament consists of spiritual grace and an external sign, where will they find anything of the kind in penance? For giving marriage this name they have no other reason than the gross ignorance of the monk; who reading in the Epistle to the Ephesians (Ephesians 5:32) the word sacrament used instead of mystery, and that concerning the secret union between Christ and his Church, transferred it to marriage. Of all these things our writings contain clear and copious demonstrations, which the good Fathers refute by the one vocable anathema. This is to, conquer without a contest, or rather to triumph without a victory!

CANON 2.

Since the Sacraments of both Testaments have the same Author, the same promises, the same truth, and the same fulfillment in Christ, we justly say that they differ from each other in external signs; but agree in those things which I have mentioned, or, in one word, in the reality. For as they are appendages of doctrine, but the substance of the doctrine is the same, so the same rule holds in regard to the Sacraments. My readers perhaps would hope understand the object of the Fathers of Trent in launching this thunderbolt, did I not briefly explain. There is a vulgar dogma of the sophists, that the Sacraments of the Mosaic law figured grace, but that ours exhibit it. We maintain that God was always true in his promises, and from the beginning figured nothing which he did not exhibit to the ancient Church in reality; for the reality of circumcision was evident under Moses. Paul testifies that they then partook of the same spiritual food and the same spiritual drink. (1 Corinthians 10:3.) What answer do they give but just that it is otherwise taught in the schools? I only touch in a few words on matters which my readers will, if they please, learn fully from our writings. Let this be the sum. From the Word of God, not from the decrees of Romanists, are we to learn what difference or resemblance there is between the Sacraments. Still we deny not that a more exuberant grace is received under the kingdom of Christ, and accordingly we are wont to note a twofold difference. First, that our Sacraments do not point out Christ at a distance, as if he were absent, but exhibit him as with the finger. Secondly, as the mode of revelation is more ample, so the communication of grace is more exuberant.

CANON 3.

Who would not face the Neptunian bolt sooner than put the inventions of men on a footing with the ordinances of Christ? We read that Baptism was recommended by Christ: we read in like manner that the Lord's Supper was recommended. (Matthew 27, 28.) Of the others we read nothing of the kind: nay, for many ages after, the doctrine of these men was unknown. There can be no doubt as to the aim and force of our Savior's question, "The baptism of John, was it from heaven or of men?" For he means that it would not be legitimate if it had not come down from heaven. Wherefore let us decide in all safety on the authority of Christ, that there is no danger in repudiating whatever has emanated merely from human authority. Not contented, however, with claiming equal authority for all, they prefer the chrism of their confirmation to the baptism of Christ! For their making one of more dignity than another is not for the purpose of placing those which have no support from Scripture in an inferior grade, but they renew those execrable blasphemies which the Council of Aurelium first vented — that we are made only half Christians by baptism, and are finished by confirmation! — and other things there delivered to the same effect.

CANON 4.

I will readily allow that the use of those things which Christ gave us as helps to salvation is necessary, that is, when an opportunity is given: although believers are always to be reminded that there is no other necessity for any sacrament than that of an instrumental cause, to which the power of God is by no means to be tied down. Every pious person must with his whole heart shudder at the expression that the things are superfluous. But here the worthy Fathers, with their usual stupidity, perceive not that whatever grace is conferred upon us by the Sacraments, is nevertheless to be ascribed to faith. He who separates faith from the Sacraments, does just as if he were to take the soul away from the body. Therefore, as we exclude not the doctrine of the gospel when we say that we obtain the grace of Christ by faith alone, so neither do we exclude the Sacraments, the nature of which is the same, as they are seals of the gospel

CANON 5.

We acknowledge that the Sacraments are intended, not only to maintain but to increase faith. But these horned gentry mean something else; for they pretend that the Sacraments have a magical power, which is efficacious without faith. This error destroys the relation which the Scriptures uniformly establish between the Sacraments and faith. That my readers may perceive this more clearly, they must always call to mind, that the Sacraments are nothing but instrumental causes of bestowing grace upon us, and are beneficial, and produce their effect only when they are subservient to faith.

CANON 6.

Here these preposterous men mix dross with silver. Wherefore we must make a distinction: — First, then, if there are any who deny that the Sacraments contain the grace which they figure, we disapprove of them. But when the horned Fathers add that the Sacraments of themselves confer grace on those not opposing any obstacle to it, they pervert the whole force of Sacraments. For they always relapse into the old delirium of the sophists, that even unbelievers receive the grace which is offered in the Sacraments, provided they do not reject it by opposing other obstacles — as if unbelief were not in itself obstacle enough. Let us hold, therefore, that we cannot obtain the grace offered in the Sacraments, unless we are capacitated by faith. What immediately follows they have appended either very maliciously, or very absurdly. They say, "as if they were only external signs;" nay, they speak as if there was no alternative between these two things. As we repudiate the monkish fiction, that the Sacraments are available in any other way than by faith, so we willingly conjoin with the signs a true exhibition of the reality, holding that they have no effect without faith, and yet that they are not empty and naked signs of a distant grace.

CANON 7.

The first thing was to define what it is duly to receive the Sacraments. For this swinish herd, passing by faith, and placing repentance in the background — not indeed that ceremonial repentance which they loudly extol, but that inward repentance of the heart, by which the whole man turns to God — think that the due receiving of the Sacraments consists in some sort of simulate devotion, as they term it. But if we were agreed as to what constitutes a legitimate disposition, there would be no farther dispute as to efficacy. For who doubts that the grace which God promises is exhibited to those who make a due approach? Hence, every one moderately instructed in the pure use of the Sacraments, will perceive that they make an absurd distinction when they say, that in so far as relates to God, grace is given, for, be the unworthiness of man what it may, God must always remain true. In respect of God, therefore, nothing is withheld or deducted from the efficacy of the Sacraments, however unbecoming the profanation of them, in respect of the evil conscience of man. The effect only is lost, or at least intercepted from coming to us.

CANON 8.

Here, indeed, they disclose their impiety, not only more clearly, but also more grossly. The device of *opus operatum* is recent, and was coined by illiterate monks, who had never learned anything of the nature of Sacraments. For in Sacraments God alone properly acts; men bring nothing of their own, but approach to receive the grace offered to them. Thus, in Baptism, God washes us by the blood of his Son, and regenerates us by this Spirit; in the Supper he feeds us with the flesh and blood of Christ. What part of the work can man claim, without blasphemy, while the whole appears to be of grace? The fact of the administration being committed to men, derogates no more from the operation of God than the hand does from the artificer, since God alone acts by them, and does the whole. But those blockheads, to say nothing of their finding human merit in the free gifts of God, pretend that we, in doing nothing, merit from God, and lay him under liability to us; and not contented with this, give vent to monstrous words to extort a confession from God, that he is not to be regarded as acting alone in the Sacraments, — hence their additional inference necessarily follows, viz., that grace is not received by faith alone. For if we grant their postulate — that grace is procured in the Sacraments *opere operato* — a part of merit is separated from faith, and the use of the Sacraments is in itself effectual for salvation. But if the same thing is to be affirmed of the Sacraments as of the word, then the Apostle is a witness that they are of no avail unless received by faith.

CANON 9.

Their fable of an indelible character is the product of the same forge. It was altogether unknown to the Primitive Church, and is more suited to magical charms than to the sound doctrine of the gospel! Therefore it will be repudiated with the same facility with which it was devised. That Baptism is not to be repeated the pious are sufficiently agreed. This, which was true of Baptism, they afterwards rashly transferred to their Confirmation and Orders. The curious sought for a reason. That they might not seem to say nothing, they contrived this fictitious impression, and now they denounce anathema against all who assent not to their figment.

CANON 10.

No sound Christian makes all men equal in the administration of Word and Sacraments, not only because all things ought to be done in the Church decently and in order, but also because, by the special command of Christ, Ministers are ordained for that purpose. Therefore, as a special call is required, no man who is not called may take the honor upon himself. Moreover, where do they find the office of baptizing enjoined on women, as they permit them to do?

CANON 11.

The lavishness with which they pour out their anathemas shows that they set little value upon them. Their prattle about, the intention of consecrating was produced by the sophists without any show of reason. This, though not tolerable, would be less grievous, if it did not utterly overthrow whatever solid comfort believers have in the Sacraments, and suspend the truth of God on the will of man: for if the intention of the minister is necessary, none of us can be certain of his Baptism — none approach the Holy Supper with sure confidence. I was baptized — if it so pleased the priest, whose good faith is no more known to me than that of any Ethiopian! Whether the promise of Christ in the Holy Supper is to be good to me, depends on the nod of a man whom I do not know. What kind of faith can it be that depends on the secret will of another? And yet this herd fear not to threaten us with windy anathemas, if we do not on the instant subscribe to such blasphemies. Such is my deference for the holy ordinance of Christ, that if some epicurean, inwardly grinning at the whole performance, were to administer the Supper to me according to the command of Christ and the rule given by him, and in due form, I would not doubt that the bread and the cup held forth by his hand are pledges to me of the body and the blood of Christ. It is painful to discuss such silliness, as when they say, "at least of doing what the Church does." Here they reach other dictates of their masters. Who that has his eyes sees not that this is just equivalent to enjoining in one word all that monks have ever dreamed ill their dens or sophists babbled in their quarrels? How stupid and absurd soever they may be, they must nevertheless be held firm and sure.

CANON 12.

AMEN.

CANON 13.

What they mean by the received and approved Rites of the Church every one is aware. Hence by this caveat they establish whatever superstitions human presumption has superinduced on the pure ordinances of

the Lord. The genuine rite of Baptism is simple, and the administration
of the Supper simple, if we look to what the Lord has enjoined. But under how many, and how various and discordant additions has this simplicity been buried? They will say, that if there is any excess, it behooves
to be rescinded — only, however, if they think so. But what hope do they
give us, when with bacchanalian fury they belch forth their anathemas
against whosoever permits himself to omit one little ceremony? All the
godly complain, or at least regret, that in Baptism more is made of the
chrism, the taper, the salt, the spittle in fine, than the washing with water,
in which the whole perfection of Baptism consists. They deplore that the
Supper has not only been vitiated by impure additions, but converted
into a kind of spurious show. According to the Fathers of Trent, nothing
can be so monstrous as not to find a place among the approved rites of
the Catholic Church. Augustine, even in his time, complained that the
Church was burdened with a Jewish bondage, though the rites then in
use were scarcely a tenth part of those the observance of which is now
more rigidly required than that of any human or divine law. The men of
Trent deliberate as to what should be done, and then, without holding
out any hope of relief, launch curses and imprecations at all who will not
submit to every iota of the usages prescribed!

ANTIDOTE TO THE CANONS ON BAPTISM.

CANON 1.

A great matter certainly to determine, that when the doctrine is the
same, the grace offered the same, and the rites observed the same, there is
a similitude. If in these three things the Baptism of Christ differs in any
respect from that of John, I admit that they have gained the day; but if
they are all common to both, in vain do they vent their bile. Nobody of
composed mind will be frightened. Had they thought that reason was to
decide, they would have been far more moderate.

CANON 2.

Why they raise a question on the former point I know not, unless perhaps this is the one only method in which they wish to be wise in checking the frivolous subtleties of the Sorbonists. But they are too passionate in fulminating against all who differ from them in the exposition of a single passage, especially when no ancient writer can be quoted who gives a metaphorical meaning to the words, "Unless men be born of water and of the Spirit." But as I said at the beginning, having a rich storehouse of execration, there is no wonder that they are liberal in dealing them out.

CANON 3.

Why did they not rather begin with this, since on this, as the foundation, they might raise any superstructure? For if all they teach is true, why are we still fighting? But our writings clearly show that the whole doctrine of Baptism, as taught by them, is partly mutilated, partly vicious. Now, while they are unable to refute our arguments, it is vain to think of hiding themselves under the flash of an anathema! When they proudly call Rome the mother and witness of all Churches, what effrontery? Did she beget in Christ the Greek and Eastern Churches, by which rather she was begotten? What teaching of hers could reach other Churches which had far more learned Bishops? Let them bring forward all the most distinguished men they have ever had, will they out of the whole catalogue produce one equal either to Cyprian, or Ambrose, or Augustine?

CANON 4.

What the Minister intends to do is of little consequence to us, provided the action itself corresponds to the genuine ordinance of Christ, both in doctrine and ritual. Let it suffice us then to have been baptized in the name of the Father, and the Son, and the Holy Spirit, whatever may have been the ignorance or impiety of those who administered Baptism to us. Man is merely the hand; it is Christ alone who truly and properly baptizes.

CANON 5.

That the unskillful may not be imposed upon, we must tell them that there is a middle place between free and necessary, in the sense in which the Romanists use the latter term. We, too, acknowledge that the use of Baptism is necessary that no one may omit it from either neglect or contempt. In this way we by no means make it free (optional.) And not only do we strictly bind the faithful to the observance of it, but we also maintain that it is the ordinary instrument of God in washing and renewing us; in short, in communicating to us salvation. The only exception we make is, that the hand of God must not be tied down to the instrument. He may of himself accomplish salvation. For when an opportunity of Baptism is wanting, the promise of God alone is amply sufficient. But of this subject something was said on a former Session.

CANON 6.

The paradox which they condemn we also repudiate, were it only for this one reason, that it extinguishes the life of faith.

CANON 7.

Did they understand what the law of Christ is, they would without difficulty agree as to the rest; but from the way in which they are wont to speak of the law of Christ, they demonstrate by this one head how far they are from the true knowledge of Baptism. Nor am I unaware what it is that has misled them. For as Paul teaches, that by circumcision a man was bound to keep the law of Moses, (Galatians 5:30) so they make out a similar obligation in Baptism in respect of the law of Christ. And the comparison would be apt did they not stumble, so to speak, on the very threshold: for they err exceedingly in thinking that Paul is there discoursing of the use and not rather of the abuse of circumcision. For if all who were circumcised were debtors to keep the whole law, it follows that they were liable to the curse. But Paul teaches very differently when he calls circumcision a seal of the righteousness of faith. (Romans 4:11.) Those who pretended that working was meritorious made a profession of keeping the law. What is Baptism to us in the present day? Although it is a deed of mutual obligation between us and God, it has this as its special property, viz., to make us certain of the free forgiveness of sins, and the perpetual gift of adoption. This is as repugnant to the affirmation of Trent as freedom is contrary to slavery.

CANON 8.

There is one Lawgiver, says James, who is able to save and to destroy. When they have, demonstrated this to be false, we will not refuse to bind ourselves by their laws. But so long as it shall appear that 'God has taken the consciences of the godly under the government of his word, and claims this as his right, we may safely conclude that there is no Holy Church which will attempt to fetter consciences by other laws.

CANON 9.

The first thing to have determined was, What are lawful vows? This being fixed, little or no dispute would remain. But now the vows under which wretched souls are put, or rather strangled, are not only full of superstition, but altogether at variance with the right rule of Christian life. Wherefore, to make any vow binding, it ought to be required at the profession of Baptism. If this be so, there is not one of the vows used in the Papacy at the present day that will not be void.

CANON 10.

Those who hold that sins are effaced by the mere remembrance of Baptism, do not mean a bare or frigid remembrance, but are conjoined with faith and repentance. Such also is the primary view of Baptism. For we ought to turn our thoughts not only to the sprinkling of water, but to the spiritual reality which begets the confidence of a good conscience by the resurrection of Christ, as Peter speaks. (1 Peter 3:21.) Such remembrance, I say, not only makes sins venial, but altogether obliterates them. Whenever the question relates to the forgiveness of sins, we must flee to Baptism, and from it seek a confirmation of forgiveness For as God reconciles us to himself by the daily promises of the gospel, so the belief and certainty of this reconciliation, which is daily repeated even to the end of life, he seals to us by Baptism. We were indeed baptized once, but there is a perpetual testimony of pardon and free propitiation in Christ. What do the venerable Fathers say? Out of the trite rhapsodies or the sophists they restrict the promises of Baptism to the past, and the moment any one has sinned, burying all remembrance of Baptism, they enjoin him to rest in the fictitious Sacrament. of Penance — as if Baptism were not itself a proper Sacrament of Penance. And still they will boast that they hold sound doctrine on the subject of Baptism, although they comprehend all its force in a momentary and evanescent promise of grace.

To the next three heads I not unwillingly subscribe. On the fourth I agree with them so far, but would wish my readers to observe what a deluge of anathemas they have poured forth. What they disapprove dropped on some occasion from Erasmus, perhaps, without much consideration. This I deny not, and yet a candid interpreter would only desire some correction in the terms, and conclude that the author of them was not fully versant in the government of the Church. No man of equity and moderation will fly at once to the terrors of an anathema.

ANTIDOTE TO THE CANONS ON CONFIRMATION.
CANON 1.

As this anathema has two edges, I hasten, in order to avoid being smitten with the former one, to declare that I am certainly not of the number of those who think that Confirmation, as observed under the Roman Papacy, is an idle ceremony, inasmuch as I regard it as one of the most deadly wiles of Satan. Let us remember that this pretended Sacrament is nowhere recommended in Scripture, either under this name or with this ritual, or this signification. Let us now hear with what titles they adorn their figment. In the name of Pope Melciades, (De Consecrat. Dist. 5,) they declare that the Spirit is given in Baptism for innocence, in Confirmation for increase of grace — that Baptism is sufficient for those who were instantly to die, but by Confirmation, those who are to prove victorious are armed so as to be able to sustain the contest. Thus one half of the efficacy of Baptism is lopt off, as if it were said in vain, that in Baptism the old man is crucified, in order that we may walk in newness of life. (Romans 6:6.) They add, besides, that though neither of the two is perfect without the other, yet Confirmation must be regarded with higher veneration than Baptism. For there is a decree of the Council of Aurelium, that no man should be deemed a Christian who has not been anointed by Episcopal unction. These words are fit to be propounded to children in sport. Sacrilege so replete with execrable blasphemy does indeed differ much from an idle ceremony.

Of the second branch of this head, what shall I say but that they have no mean idea of the effect which their anathemas are to have: they pour them forth as readily as if they thought they are immediately to make white black. But the truth is, that from the wonder or rather stupor with which they have seen their mysteries hitherto regarded by the vulgar, they have imagined that all their babble will be similarly received. Hence their exceeding confidence. Never would they have ventured to expose their absurdities to the judgment of the rudest hind had they not hoped that the mask of Council would, hoodwink all eyes.

CANON 2.

The question is, whether oil, the moment after they have been pleased to call it Chrism, receives, at the will of man, a new and secret virtue, of the Spirit? Oil is not mentioned by any ancient Christian writer, nay, not even by any one of that middle age wherein numerous errors abounded. Let them do what they may, therefore, they will gain nothing by denying that they insult the Spirit of God when they transfer his virtue to filthy oil.

CANON 3.

Of a truth the horned and mitred herd are worthy of such a privilege. For what could they do, seeing they are no fitter to execute the Episcopal office than hogs are to sing? Verily I do not envy them; only let them confine their impurities to their taverns, and keep them out of the Church of God. But how, pray, will they prove that this office is more befitting Bishops than other priests, unless that it hath so pleased some unknown authors? If a reason be sought from Scripture, all confess that it makes no distinction between a Bishop and a Presbyter. Then Paul is enjoined to receive imposition of hands from Ananias who was one of the disciples. (Acts 9:17.) If imposition of hands is their Confirmation, why do they not charge God with violating orders, and so profaning a mystery by confounding Presbyter and Bishop? In short, their doctrine is sanctioned either by a law of God or by human decree. If by a law of God, why are they not afraid to violate it? For they give Presbyters a right to confirm on extraordinary occasions.

While they thus thunder away in behalf of a human decree, who will be afraid?

ANTIDOTE TO THE SUBSEQUENT CANONS ON RESI-DENCE.

I sometimes wonder how it happens that, in such light of the gospel, they are just as absurd as they were wont to be in the thickest darkness. But I immediately turn to reflect on the admirable judgment of God, by which it is certain that they are so blinded and stupified, that, lost both to sight and feeling, they cast away all shame, and glory unblushingly in their own disgrace. Since the provisions of the Church, which were destined for the maintenance of pastors long ago, have begun to be the revenues of idle men, and those who are maintained at the expense of the Church think that no obligation lies upon them, they profess to have prepared themselves for the correction of this great iniquity. When they enter upon the subject they seem to say something. Where corruption is so rampant, it is, I admit, no small matter that two bishoprics are not to be held by one man. And there are other things of a similar nature, framed to curb the licentiousness which now stalks abroad, although in any reformation which they attempt, they are far, I say not from the primitive and austerer discipline which flourished a thousand years ago, but from any tolerable state of pious and well ordered government. They forbid a Bishop to absent himself from his diocese for more than half a year. The leave is liberal enough which gives six months vacation out of twelve to those who ought to watch continually over the flock, both day and night. But even here a reservation is added — unless they have a just excuse for absence. When will they be without such excuse? And yet, supposing they most strictly observe what is here prescribed, what benefit will result, unless, perhaps, that they will not be able to career out of the district all the money which the living yields? If they love the city, they will have their palaces where, away from all noise, they will drink, play, and sleep as usual; if they prefer the country, they will have pleasant retreats in their seats and castles. Thus they will perform their office doing nothing, and yet giving actual residence.

As to parishes, they confirm schools in their privileges, so that the pretext of studying will excuse absence. Meanwhile, while the young and raw tyro learns to act the pastor, will he nevertheless draw the milk of the flock which will be left without a pastor. Grant that this may be tolerated, yet who knows not that lazy scullions alone enjoy the privileges of the Schools? The consequence will be, that the miserable churches will be forced to rear two wolves, one at home and another abroad. The resolution not to give effect in future to dispensations *de non promovendo*, beyond a year, was, I shrewdly guess, suggested by the granters. For what all addition will be made to their gains, if a new prerogative shall require to be purchased every year? In short, their only care seems to have been to exhibit some show of justice in a state of universal confusion.

But even if their regulations had been perfect to a title, good men could not congratulate themselves on the prospect of a better state of matters. For before they enact any law they abrogate all laws together, by one word, or at least point out a method by which they may all be abrogated: for they promise that none of the things which they may say are to hinder the Apostolic See from maintaining its authority unimpaired. Now, let any one consider with himself by what limits that authority is bounded, or how far it extends. Does not a preliminary of this kind just mean, that the Popes may order anything to be lawful that they please? What remedy, pray, do they bring by so acting? None of the things which they undertake to correct have hitherto been practiced as if permitted by common law, but what the laws prohibited was done with impunity by means of dispensations. Accordingly, those guilty of abuses never alleged that they observed the, strict rule, but having been set free from law, they thought they might do what otherwise in itself was not lawful. The

Neptunian fathers now provide that the future shall be no better, by making a special proviso that the power of the Roman Court shall suffer no diminution. For though a thousand knots of laws were tied, the sword of Alexander is unsheathed to cut them all at once. Could they more openly mock the Christian world. Why do I say mock? Could they more grossly insult the expectation of the good, than when they deliver thus distinctly, and with barbarian haughtiness, that they will set no bounds to the unbridled tyranny of the Pope?

Callous as those who live under the Papacy have become to all evils, it might be said that on this one matter they had forgotten their bondage, I mean, in not only freely lamenting but crying aloud that the Church was ruined by dispensations. All eyes were turned to the venerable Fathers, sitting like strict and zealous censors to check the abuse. After pondering for eighteen months they declare their approval of ancient discipline, provided the Roman See retain its right of dispensing as before. In other words, the laws are to be so far enforced that liberty to violate them shall not be gratuitous, but may be purchased. And that the Pope may not be prevented by modesty from boldly exercising the power, they confirm him in the title of Universal Bishop, which Gregory calls nefarious, blasphemous, abominable, and the forerunner of Antichrist, while they leave nothing more to the Bishops than to be his Vicars. Where is that equality which Jerome heralds when he compares the Bishop of Rome to the Bishop of Eugubium? (Hierom. ad Evag.) Where is the doctrine of Cyprian that the Bishopric of Christ is one, and part of it is held entire (*in solidum*) by each Bishop? (Cyp. de Simplic. Prelat.) Bernard writes that it was a common complaint in his time, that the Churches were maimed and mutilated, because the Roman Bishop by drawing all power to himself confounded orders, (Bernard. de Consid. ad Eng. lib. 3.) To cure this evil the Holy Council bids Bishops be the Vicars of the Pope.

I will spend no more time in exposing their impudence. But as all see that they are worse than hopeless, every one who is wise wilt in future disregard their decrees, and be in no dubiety about them. It were indeed most desirable that the dissensions by which the Church is now disturbed should be settled by the authority of a pious Council, but as matters are we cannot yet hope for it. Therefore, since Churches are scattered in a dreadful manner, and no hope of gathering them together appears from man, each cannot do better than hasten to rally round the banner which the Son of God holds out to us. This is not a time to keep waiting for one another. As every one sees the light of Scripture beaming forth, let him instantly follow. In regard to the whole body of the Church, we commend it to the care of its Lord. Meanwhile, let us not be either slothful or secure. Let each do his best. Let us contribute whatever in us is of counsel, learning, and abilities, to build up the ruins of the Church. But, in affairs so desperate, let us be sustained and animated by the promise that, as none appears from among men to undertake the once with manly and heroic mind, The Lord, armed with His own justice and with the weight of His own arm, will Himself alone perform all things.